ASPECTS OF AGRARIAN AND URBAN HISTORY OF THE MARATHAS

Aspects of Agrarian and Urban History of the Marathas

ISBN : 81-7169-162-5

Edition : 2024

Published by :
COMMONWEALTH PUBLISHERS (P) LTD.
4831/24, Govind Lane,
Ansari Road, Darya Ganj,
New Delhi - 110002
Ph. : 23272541, 23242541
e-mail : commonwealthpublishers2016@gmail.com

Distributed by :
ARJUN PUBLISHING HOUSE
4831/24, Govind Lane,
Ansari Road, Darya Ganj,
New Delhi - 110002
Ph. : 23272541, 23242541
e-mail : arjunbooks2001@gmail.com

Laser Typesetting by :
Dimple Computers
Delhi

Printed at :
Divine Digital Printers
Delhi

Aspects of Agrarian and Urban History of the Marathas

T.T. MAHAJAN

Commonwealth

Dedicated to

Shri Sureshbhai M. Patel,
Honourable President of
Gram Vikas Sanstha, Saraswati Vidya Mandir,
Primary School, Arts and Commerce Junior
Mahavidyalaya, Sarvajanik Vachanalaya,
Sane Guruji Backward Class Hostel, etc., Bamkhede,
And Respectable Principal
of S.P.D.M. College, Shirpur,
as a token of gratitude and affection.

Preface

The present monogragh on Aspects of Agrarian and Urban History of the Marathas is a selection from my research papers presented at All India History Conferences and National Seminars on Indian history. Some of them have been written exclusively for the present work. Some papers have appeared in regional periodicals and other Research Journals. The papers published earlier have been now examined and reviewed by incorporating additional information in them. Therefore, one can find them, in present form as slightly altered. I am indeed thankful to the editors of the periodicals in which following research articles throwing light on the various aspects of agrarian and urban history of Maratha country in the 17th and the 18th centuries have appeared prior to the publication of this study:

1. Rise of Maratha Power : An Economic Perspective (Itihasacharya V.K. Rajwade, Sanshodhan Mandal's Periodical "Sanshodhak", September, 1988, Part 3).
2. Food Prices and Economic Condition during Shivaji's period (1630-1707) ('Sanshodhak', Itihasacharya V. K. Rajwade, Sanshodhan Mandal's Periodical, January, 1982, Part 4).
3. Famine Policy of the Maratha State (Studies on Shivaji and his Times, Shivaji University Publication, 1982).

4. Agricultural Technology in Maratha Country, 17th and 18th Centuries (Sanshodhak, December, 1984).
5. Urbanization in Maharashtra during the 17th Century (Sanshodhak, March, 1985).
6. Urbanization in Maharashtra during the 18th Century (Proceedings of Forty Fourth Session of Indian History Congress, Burdwan, 1983).
7. Urban Social Mobility in Maharashtra in the 18th Century (Proceedings of Forty Fifth Session of Indian History Congress, Annamalai, 1984).

Following research papers were read at the History Conferences :

1. Some Aspects of Agrarian Change in the 18th Century Maharashtra, Paper read in I.C.H.R. Seminar on "Agrarian Relations in Medieval Deccan", University of Poona, 12th to 16th of March, 1985.
2. Textile Industry of Paithan in the 18th Century, Paper read in U.G.C. National Seminar on the Personality of Paithan, Paithan, 25th to 27th February, 1988.
3. Rural Problems in Konkan in the 17th Century, Paper read in I.C.H.R. Seminar on "Western India: State, Economy and Society, 1600-1900", University of Bombay, 7-9 January, 1988.
4. Social Barriers and Communal Harmony between the Hindus and the Muslims in Maratha Country, Paper read in Maharashtra History Conference, held at Dayanand College, Solapur, 27-29 January, 1986.
5. Social Groups and Relations in Towns in Maratha Country with special reference to Poona, Paper read in the Indian History Congress, Amritsar, 1985.
6. Forts, Monasteries, and Pilgrimages : Factors of Urbanization in the 17th Century Maratha Kingdom, Paper prepared for presenting it in

International Seminar on Indian History, Shivaji University, Kolhapur, Sept., 1987.

The preparation of the present monograph could not have been possible without the help and assistance rendered by the Librarian and the staff of Deccan College, Pune, the Secretary Bharat Itihas Sanshodhan Mandal, Pune, who have permitted me to use valuable source material in their possession. I express my deep sense of gratitude to Annasaheb V.T. Randhir, the President of K.V.P. Sanstha, Shirpur and Shri S.M. Patel, Principal of S.P.D.M. College, Shirpur, for their encouragement and necessary help for completing this work. I am thankful to Shri D.B. Patil, the Librarian and the staff of our library who helped me in providing the Library facilities. Without the help and inspiration of my beloved wife Suman, daughter Manisha, and two sons, Prashant and Sachin, this work would not be completed. Last but not the least, I must thank Shri R.V. Patil, for meticulous typing of the book.

Dr. T.T. MAHAJAN

Abbreviations

AA	Angrekalin Ashtagar
SPSS	Shivkalin Patrasar Sangraha
MIS	Marathyanchya Itihasachi Sadhane
SCS	Shiv Charitra Sahitya
SKPSS	Sambhajikalin Patrasar Sangraha
PD	Peshwa Daftar
Peshwa Diaries	Selections from Satara Raja's and Peshwa Diaries
PS	Peshwaichya Sawalit
PSAP	Peshwekalin Samajik Va Arthik Patravyavahar
SVD	Selections from Vaidya Daftar
PNSV	Pune Nagar Sanshodhan Vritta
PKM	Peshwekalin Maharashtra
ERS	English Records on Shivaji
FBS	Foreign Biographies of Shivaji

Contents

1

Introduction

The present volume is based upon my original investigation appeared in research papers contributed by myself to the various periodicals and regional journals of history during the last ten years. Those research papers represent various aspects of the agrarian and urban history of Maratha Kingdom during the 17th and the 18th centuries. They help us in understanding the social relations between the different social groups of the towns in the 18th century Maharashtra.

Some of the pages in the work also throw a light on different aspects of the changing conditions of agriculture in Maratha Kingdom during the 17th and the 18th centuries. They also depict an interesting picture of social harmony between the Hindu-Muslim communities in Maratha Kingdom.

The subject that deals with the important historical event of Shivaji's rise to power on which earlier scholars have made their contribution to the discussion of its socio-political and religious background, has also been attempted from different point of view. The discussion on the economic conditions prevailed in Maharashtra under the Deccan Muslim Sultans and that favoured the rise of Maratha Power during the 17th century, has been presented for the first time. The earlier scholars seem to have ignored to analyse the economic factor facilitating the rise of Shivaji's political movement in Maharashtra. In the present study the subject has been reconsidered by applying a new approach of the economic forces causing to provoke the Maratha reaction against the Muslim powers in the Deccan. Thus the discussion throws a different light on the major event that took place in the political history of Maharashtra of the 17th century.

The discussion on communal harmony between the Hindus and the Muslims in Maratha country reveals a complete picture of the communal tension and also the Hindu-Muslim unity of those times. It appropriately describes the relationship between Hindu-Muslim communities during the Maratha rule. Ultimately the discussion sheds a considerable light on the attitude of religious toleration of the Maratha rulers and their contribution towards the communal harmony between the Hindus and the Muslims, which ultimately resulted in fostering of the assimilation of two cultures of both communities in Maharashtra of the period under review.

Economic Background of the Rise of Maratha Power

The seventeenth century represents a crucial period in the history of Maharashtra. It saw the collapse of Nizamshahi and Adilshahi kingdoms in Deccan. The major event during this century is certainly the rise of political movement under Shivaji's leadership. The recent studies[1] throw a light on political, social and religious circumstances which favoured the rise of Maratha power. Some of the works explain the phenomenal rise of the Marathas in the 17th century by referring the political events and their traditions in the past.[2] While others enable us to understand the social background to the rise of Maratha movement.[3] The importance of Shivaji's rise to power cannot be better realised unless the economic conditions prevailed in Maharashtra in the 16th and at the beginning of the 17th century is properly understood.

The present discussion gives us a clear understanding of economic background in which King Shivaji rose to power. It makes a brief survey of economic forces which also caused more or less the Marathas to unite and give their support to Shivaji's attempt of throwing off Muslim yoke.

Economic Exploitation of the People

To the people, the Deccan Muslim rulers provided no facilities for a better economic future or brought no progress in economic fields. The economic distress of the Hindu subjects in Deccan can be observed in the confiscation of their lands and properties by the Deccan Sultans, their exploitation in matter of oppressive taxation, and forced labour exacted from them etc. The oppressive and discriminative policy of the Sultans in taxation made the Hindus miserable and was sure to irritate the disgruntled elements in them. We find many evidences to the ruthless economic exploitation of the Hindus by the Muslim Sultans, their officials and watandars. After the Muslim conquests, the lands and the watans of some of the Hindus in Maharashtra were confiscated by the Muslims. For instance, the lands belonging to the Hindus, the inhabitants in Konkan reign, were captured by the newly converted Muslim communities like Arab and Habsi.[4] While some of the Muslims, forcibly made the Hindus to abandon their watans,[5] and by confiscating those watans they became the watandars. The property of the Hindus at Dabhol was confiscated by the Bijapuri Sultan, when they died without leaving the sons.[6] The wealth and property of a Hindu person, the son of Peda Redi was plundered and confiscated by the Sultan of Golkonda.[7] The inam lands of some of the Hindus were also confiscated by the State in the reign of Muhammad Adilshah.[8] This resulted in weakening their economic position and made them poorer. Some of the Deccan Sultans exploited the distressed Hindus by making discrimination when foodgrain was sold to them. For instance, the foodgrain during the period of scarcity was sold by Government at cheaper rates only to the Muslims and not to the Hindus in the reign of Bahmani king, Sultan Muhammad.[9] The Hindus were exploited economically, by making distinction between the Hindus and the Muslims in the matter of taxation also. The Muslims enjoyed the tax and tariff concessions. Accordingly the Muslims whenever required to pay, paid the custom duty at the low rate of 2½% and the Hindus paid the tax at the higher rate[10] of 5%. Moreover, the latter had to pay 13% as stamping duty and brokerage in addition to 5% custom duty.[11] The Government officers like hawaldar at the port also demanded for presents and forced loans as the price of his favour from the Hindu merchants.[12] The oppressive duties increased the annual income from custom duty at Bijapuri ports like Rajapur and Chaul to Rs. 24,000 and Rs. 15,000 respectively.[13]

The Hindus were compulsorily made to pay full taxes while the Muslims got total exemption from them.[14] The Muslim men also denied the loan to be paid by them and borrowed from a Hindu banker on the false complaint against the latter that he cursed the Muslim person or Islam.[15] This tendency certainly reduced the Hindu banker to the brink of bankruptcy. Again if a Muslim revenue officers demanded silver from a Hindu, the latter had to give him gold with all respect and humanity.[16] It is obvious from the above evidences that the Muslims obtained considerable concessions and economic advantages than the Hindus.

Economic Loss of People

Under the regime of Deccan Sultans, people were depressed a lot economically. To the most of Hindus, the Governments of Deccan Muslim states mean serious economic blows, paralysing the whole Hindu society. Though the majority of the inhabitants of Deccan Muslim kingdoms was of the Hindus, they had no voice in the governments which were dominated by the Muslim class consisting of foreign immigrants (Pardesis), the Deccanis and the Indian converts. Majority of Hindu population derived their livelihood from the agriculture, whereas all the Muslims practically depended for their livelihood on the state.[17] With few exceptions, the Hindus were employed on only subordinate or minor administrative posts and they were not given the post of governor, military commander or even a minister in the Bijapur kingdom.[18] Peasants and many other lower castes of Hindus such as Ramoshis, Berads, Kolis, Bhandaris, Mahars, Mangs etc., who served the agrarian community were excluded from high ranks and positions and were used as forced labour for constructing Government buildings and public works. It is, however, not untrue that some of the Maratha nobles like Bhosles, Nimbalkars, Ghorpades, Shirkes, Mores, Mohites, Ghatges, and such others obtained power and posts of trust and responsibility at the courts of Adilshahs as well as other Deccan Sultans and acquired the jagirs.[19] The high caste men among the Hindus like Brahmins were too employed in revenue and account departments of the states.[20] But they were a few in number. Only noble men enjoyed the life of richness, absolute power and common people in Deccan lived a miserable life.[21] Again there was none among the Hindus who by involving in trade as well as by establishing trading contacts with neighbouring and foreign states[22], could become prosperous, probably because of the oppressive and discriminative policy of the Sultans regarding the tax on trade. Thus, as the subjects, Hindus were the losers economically.

It is also reflected in the observations of foreign travellers who visited Deccan in the 15th and 16th centuries, that the Hindus lived in conditions of extreme poverty even during the normal period. Nikitin, a Russian merchant says that the Hindus of Deccan were all naked and barefooted.[23] Barbosa[24], who was a witness to the gloomy conditions of the Hindus in Deccan says that they went naked from waist upwards and wore small turbans on their heads.

Linchosten also observed the deplorable condition of cultivating classes in Deccan.[25] The foregoing discussion tries to search out the different factors responsible for the prevalence of poverty in Deccan Muslim kingdoms.

Factors Contributing to the Poverty of the Hindu Subjects of the Deccan Muslim Sultans

The taxation policy of Adilshahi and Nizamshahi

Sultans contributed to the general poverty condition of the mass of the people. The revenue assessment in Deccan Muslim kingdoms was not based on any careful calculation. It was formed out and varied from region to region,[26] hence the subjects could be oppressed to certain extent.[27] The land revenue collected by the Jagirdars was heavy which was usually half of the total produce.[28] The people suffered greatly due to exaction of the collectors of the jagirdars.[29] Burnell also supports that the share of the state in produce of land in south India was one-half of the gross produce.[30] In Nizamshahi under Malik Ambar, the rate of assessment was two-fifth of the produce of government land and one-fourth of the yield of other land[31] The cultivators were obliged to pay their revenue even if the land was not cultivated. They had to bear all the risks of failures and destructions of harvests.[32] In Golkonda kingdom, the government demand was one-half of the agricultural produce.[33] According to Moreland, during the 16th century the revenue demand was substantially higher in the South than in North and the peasants in Deccan were probably worse than those in Mughal territory.[34] The revenue tax in the lands of jagirdars was even worse oppressive than the case of the lands of crown.[35] The watandar Deshmukhs, Deshkulkarnis with the grants of the lands also claimed some taxes in form of annual supply of shoes, oil vegetables, cloths, etc., from members of village society.[36] And very often they extracted more revenue than what was due from peasants[37], and plundered their property, houses also.[38] The jagirdar of Kasba Trimbak in Sangamner Sarkar when exacted Rs. 4000 the unlawful collection from the peasantry, the latter protested against his act to the king.[39] The watandars or government officials also exploited the merchants in local markets by compelling them to sell the commodities at low prices. Thus, Bahlulkhan Lodi, an amir of Bijapur brought pressure on the merchants with the help of local hawaldars and purchased the articles at very cheaper rates.[40] It was therefore usual for peasants in face of such oppressiveness to give up cultivation, abandon their original locality and migrate to places where such experiences did not occur. For example the Hindus in the territories of jagirdars of Nizamshah suffered much on account of heavy taxation and rigorous collection and hence abandoned the pargana of Newasa and migrated to other province.[41] Likewise, the people in kasba Poona were harassed by the officer of Adilshah who confiscated their farms and destroyed their plantation and ultimately made them to abandon the territory.[42]

The poll tax like Jiziya was compulsorily collected from the Hindus in Deccan. Ali Adilshah I[43] and Muhammad Adilshah II[44], forcefully made the Hindus to pay the Jiziya. Ali Adilsha II, compulsorily collected tribute and jiziya from the Hindu men and Zamindars like Bhadra Naik of Bednur.[45] But the Hindus in Deccan Muslim kingdoms were unable to pay the tax on account of poverty. And whenever the people were asked for jiziya, they ran away and abandoned their houses and villages.[46] The official records show that jiziya was equivalent to 4 per cent;[47] and it was annually collected at the rate varied from 12½ to 28 jitals in Adilshahi kingdom in the reign of Muhammad Adilshah.[48] According to Manucci, the Hindu rich merchants had to pay 13½ rupees, the middle class had to pay 6¼ rupees, and poor paid 3½ rupees every year. The Muslim officers who collected jiziya were offensive and insulted the Hindus when they collected the tax[49] from the latter. Thus, economically the Hindus were suppressed by the Deccan Muslim rulers.

Burden of Taxation

The peasants in addition to revenue tax gave the share of produce to the watandars in form of their rights such as Halipatti[50], Pestarpatti, and Bajepatti, for their services. The Baluta dues were to be paid by every farmer to each Balutedar.[51] Besides this, not less than fifty different types of cesses (abwabs) were prevalent [52] Among them were included the tax on tobacco, customs,[53] bhet, paiposhi,[54] selbail,[55] Sarafipatti,[56] bittobigar, zaripilgi, Jangtin, Mohimpatti,[57] Zari-Imarat, Mizabani,[58] Farmaishi, Faski, Nawsil Bail, etc., which were collected from the people. The tax of Ambarjakati was also imposed on the people.[59] The rate of this tax varied from village to village. It was lower on small village and higher on the big village.[60] War indemnity or peshkash (gifts) were other form of forcefully exactions from the peasants by the Sultans. An indemnity[61] of 18 lacs on Adilshah and 12 lacs on Nizamshah was imposed by the Mughals in 1621. In 1624, Malik Ambar who agreed to pay indemnity to the Mughals went to Kandhar and collected the amount of tribute by plundering the territories as well as by forcefully exacting from peasants of Golkonda.[62] Mr. Lanepool estimates that at the accession of Aurangzeb the tribute from Adilshah and Qutubshah of Deccan was about 19 crores of rupees.[63] Thus the tribute and other forcefully exactions from peasants show the exploitation of the producers by the Sultans. It is also obvious that the burden of taxation fell more heavily on the poor classes and the mass of the people being economically suppressed, were living in the greatest poverty and distress.

The heavy taxes also indicate that royal officials, watandars, who forced the peasants to cultivate the land enjoyed the fruits of production and lived at the expense of poor sections in society. The oppressiveness of officials, watandars exploited the poor Hindus in all kinds of ways and coercive power of Deccan Muslim Sultans was behind that brutal exploitation.

Plunder of Wealth

The plunder of wealth in Maharashtra made by the invaders from 13th to 17th century was notable. During the 13th century Alauddin Khalji when attacked the rich province of Deogiri, carried off a huge booty[64] consisted of 60 maunds of gold, 7 maunds of pearls, rubies, diamonds,[65] thousand maunds of silver and other precious products of the Deccan. The Sultan Muhammad Khalji of Malwa also plundered and collected the booty from Bijapuri territories in the 15th century.[66] The rich provinces in Khandesh like Nandurbar, Sultanpur etc., were plundered by the Sultan Malik Nasir[67] and Changizkhan[68] of Gujrat in the 15th and 16th century, respectively, and a large booty was collected from those territories.[69] Ibrahim Adilshah[70] collected considerable booty by plundering the territories of Nizamshah in the 16th century. The Mughals also when plundered the territories in Deccan Muslim kingdoms looted the houses, the property of the merchants as well as of the common people.[71] The Mughal army under Khan Jahan when attacked Kandhar, Nanded, Solapur, Kolhapur, Junnar etc., the territories belonging to Nizamshah plundered the booty equivalent to 20 lacs in jewels, elephants etc., from those provinces in the 17th century.[72] Thus, the huge booty collected from various territories in Maharashtra by the invaders not only served as a factor adversely affecting the economic strength of the kingdom but also contributed to general poverty condition of the mass of the people.

Exhausted Agronomy and Trade

Famines and wars were other influential factors which exhausted the agronomy and trade of Adilshahi and Nizamshahi kingdoms. The Deccan turned out to be the battleground where Nizamshahi and Adilshahi armies' generals struggled not only against each other but also among their nobles. The constant wars[73] and plunder of villages by the enemy[74] not only wiped out the agricultural system and trade in Deccan but also completely shattered to economic life of the people. It is obvious from the writings of the Portuguese historian, Paria-Y-Suza that the trade of South India in 1566 was declined due to the wars between Vijaynagar rulers and Deccan Muslim Sultans.[75] Likewise, the conflict between Adilshah and the Portuguese finally resulted in sacking and burning of the ports in Adilshahi kingdom and imposed restrictions on the trade between Bijapur and the Portuguese at Goa.[76] Likewise, the English attack on the port of Dabhol of Bijapur in early 17th century made the conditions insecured for trade of that port and finally resulted in the decline of Dabhol from 1620 and opened the way to the final rise of Surat.[77] The disturbed conditions in Nizamshahi kingdom also resulted in closing down the market places like Rustamabad in Mamle Chaul under Nizamshahi rule.[78] All the trade in South was at a stand due to the rivalries among the rulers in South India in the year of 1643.[79] Moreover, the famines visiting the provinces in Adilshahi and Nizamshahi kingdoms at periodical intervals by damaging the agricultural produce, caused much sufferings to the people and were also responsible for breaking down the agro-economy of the Muslim kingdoms. The famine conditions compelled many people to leave their houses in search of food elsewhere,[80] on account of which numerous villages were depopulated. But it is a regretting that peasants obtained no active help or famine reliefs from Deccan Muslim rulers. For instance, during the famine year of 1630-31, Nizamshah was not at the residential place and was shifted to Aurangabad.[81] The people in his kingdom therefore believed that the natural calamities like famines were brought by the tyrannical rule of the Sultan.[82] The economic crisis thus, caused by natural calamities and wars not only ruined the agricultural production but also withheld the revenue payments. Thus, the arrears from land assessment in provinces of Ahmednagar, Khandesh, Berar, Daulatbad etc., after 1636 were considerable. The actual yield from land revenue of those provinces was only a fraction of their nominal revenue, sometimes only one-tenth of the total assessment.[83] And this seriously weakened the economic position of the Muslim states in South. In order to fill the gap between the expenditure and diminishing revenues, the Sultans, their officials, Jagirdars etc., resorted to the imposition of illegal taxes,[84] additional taxes,[85] and the plunder of houses, property[86] of peasants as well as the plunder of the Hindu temples which was one of the sources of income of the Deccan Muslim state.[87] The arrears of revenue amount made the government officials to demand forced loans,[88] and extortion of large sums from the merchants.[89] These acts no doubt added to the miserable conditions of the rayats.

Among the cottage industries, weaving industries[90] survived in some parts of Bijapuri kingdom, and it was heavily taxed. The tax in kind as well in cash was collected from the weavers.[91] As a result, many artisans in some localities left those places and went elsewhere for livelihood.[92] Likewise, the wars in the Deccan also became obstacles to such industries. In some places, the conditions of artisans became insecure both for their property and life. So for want of security they ran away from the towns to other ports like Bombay for shelter and settled there.[93] The lack of large scale industries[94] and decline in agriculture and trade[95] of Deccan Muslim kingdoms ultimately resulted in devastation of backbone of State economy.

The economic position of the people was again worsened by the corruption of government officials who harassed them in every way by indulging in evil practices. One of the important reasons for Shivaji's success to consolidate his state's position in Deccan was the inability of Adilshahi Sultan to prevent corrupt practices weakening the administrative control over the state. Shivaji made some of the Bijapuri nobles favourable to him and demoralised them through bribery. This certainly contributed to his early victory in securing some of the forts and territories belonging to Bijapur.[96]

Peasants were made to work as Bitto Begari[97] or forced labour utilising for erecting public buildings, royal palaces, courts[98] etc. Many times, Bitto Begari also became obstacle to the cultivation. For the farmers working as forced labour could not cultivate their lands and those lands remained uncultivated, unwatered,[99] and thus state income was lost. The agriculture in those days remained unprogressive due to unfavourable environment as well as due to the indifference of the Deccan Muslim rulers which they showed in bringing about the agrarian reforms. Moreover, the Sultans were not more intent on utilising the natural resources of the kingdom for the welfare of the people and finally those resources had been considerably depleted.[100]

Indebtedness of Peasantry

The heavy land assessment, frequent occurrence of famines caused rural indebtedness[101] and compelled many cultivators to borrow loan from the bankers usually the Shete-

Mahajans.[102] Many times, the debt became double and increased beyond the paying capacity of peasants.[103] The absence of any other source of income except cultivation, the lack of production, uncertainty of rains, inefficiency of tillage technique, high rate of interest,[104] all these brought limitations on peasant's ability to repay the debts. As a result their debts increased day by day and compelled them to sell their property of houses[105] and lands.[106] The indebtedness of peasantry caused many of them to forcefully abandon their homes and villages,[107] and reduced them to beggary.

Prices, Wages and Standard of Living

For attempting the description of standard of life prevailing in Maharashtra before Shivaji's rise to power, nothing like a systematic price-data is available. For the treatment of that subject, one has to depend upon the prices prevailing in other neighbouring Muslim state.[108] From those price data one can form some idea of standard of living of common people in the territory and of the period with which we are dealing. In the following table, prices prevailed in Deccan Muslim kingdom are compared with those in Maratha kingdom under Shivaji.

Prices prevalent in Deccan Muslim kingdom			*Prices prevalent in Maratha kingdom under Shivaji*		
Grains	*Weight in Maund*[109]	*Price per rupee*	*Grains*	*Weight in Maund*	*Price per rupee*
Rice	1 to 1½[110]	—	Rice	2½[111]	—
Wheat	1/2[112]	—	Wheat	1½[113]	—

From the above table, it appears that on the average the food prices in Deccan Muslim kingdoms were certainly higher. They were two or three times cheaper in Maratha kingdom under Shivaji than those prevailing in the Muslim kingdoms. The wages were very low.[114] If we take for granted that the cost of living in medieval India was roughly 5 takas or 5 rupees per month,[115] then it is obvious that a person of our period whose monthly income was less than 5 rupees, could hardly get two meals a day and he had no ulternative than to face the starvation. Thus, the picture drawn on above rough calculations is not much different from the one drawn on the basis of the accounts of foreign travellers. The economic conditions of the people in Nizamshahi and Adilshahi kingdoms was in no way better. The Deccan Muslim regimes thus marked not only by continuous wars or struggles but also by the features of economic chaos such as poverty, shadow of famines, destruction of agricultural crops, plunders of wealth, illegal exactions, oppression of peasants by the watandars and finally the starvation of the masses.

It is in this circumstance that the emergence of Shivaji to the political power must be viewed. It is beyond doubt that the poverty enabled the oppressed peasants and lower sections in society to rise and remove the yoke of exploitation, and stimulated them to give their support to Shivaji who had started building up a movement of resistance to the Deccan Muslim rulers. The Marathas supported the cause of Shivaji with the desire that their economic conditions would improve under the new rule of their own king.[116] Promotion of economic prosperity[117] of the people was one of the primary motives of Shivaji. This is abundantly clear from a number of his orders[118] and instructions[119] given to the officers for avoiding illegal exactions[120] of extra taxes[121] from the peasants. It has often been suggested that the revolution brought about by Shivaji was primarily political and more social than economic. But a close scrutiny of the contemporary sources however suggests that the political revolution of Shivaji not only aimed at giving liberty, protection to the people,[122] and their religion, but also motivated by the economic interests. It had some economic base,[123] formed on certain principles of economic prosperity of the subjects.

Demand to the Agricultural Frodaction in Kingdom of Shivaji in Overseas Markets

We notice that the agricultural products in Shivaji's kingdom which were in demand in the markets of Middle East played an important role in foreign trade of his country. Various types of agricultural products in his Swaraj such as rice, wheat, pepper, cotton, betelnuts, cocoanuts,[124] opium etc., were carried out to the ports like Cheul, Rajapur, Dabhol, Vengurla, Cambay for their export to Eden, Bassara, Mocha, Muscat and other parts of Middle East.[125] Among the notable agricultural products exported from the Maratha kingdom to the foreign countries was pepper. Rajapur, and adjoining territories of it, in Konkan region produced pepper abundantly. The English at Rajapur had stored a huge quantity of pepper in their factory at the town.[126] The English merchants at this port exported three thousand Khandies of pepper, near one thousand tons, every year to the foreign territories. The Bania merchants at Bombay also procured a large quantity of pepper at Rajapur and loaded their ships with the goods like pepper and sent them to European countries. It was estimated in 1673 that the vessel loaded with pepper at Rajapur was worth above eighty or ninety thousand rupees.[127]

It is ovious from export trade of pepper by the British merchants at Bombay[128] who procured it at Rajapur, that the pepper produced in the Maratha kingdom had good demand in the foreign markets of Bassara, Hormuz and the ports of Red Sea etc., where the English ships were unloaded every year. Next agricultural product in the kingdom of Shivaji that was in great demand was the cotton. Cotton was produced on large quantity in southern parts of Maratha country. The coarse cloth was manufactured at Rajapur. The Bania merchants at Bombay purchased the cloths from the English at the place of Rajapur.[129] It appears that Shivaji's ambassador had brought several sorts of cloth for selling them to the English at Bombay.[130] Raybag found to be a place where cotton was produced on considerable scale. The English at Raybag sent the cloths manufactured at that place to Bombay for their export to European countries.[131] The factors at Rajapur reported that various sorts of cloths in the Deccan were procured at cheaper rates at Rajapur than they were procurable at Surat.[132] Cocoanut was other important product that was in circulation in the external markets ot the East and West countries. The territory of western coast of Shivaji's kingdom produced cocoanuts abundantly. The English purchased them on large scale from the Marathas.[133] The King Shivaji who was indebted to the British company due to the goods purchased by him from the English could not repay the debt in cash. Therefore, he declared to return it to the English by supplying them the quantity of agricultural products of cocoanuts, betelnuts etc.[134]

The English had procured a good number of cocoanuts and one hundred maunds of betelnuts from Shivaji in 1677, for exporting them to foreign markets.[135] In 1679, the English agents at Rajapur purchased two hundred ninety two khandies of betelnuts and 500,000 cocoanuts for exporting them to Bombay.[136] The European merchants like the English took a great interest in betelnut that was of great demand in external markets. The Konkan region in his territory supplied betelnuts on large quantity to the European merchants in India In 1676, Shivaji had supplied them a huge quantity of cocoanuts and betelnuts, for loading five vessels belonging to the English.[137] In 1677, the English received a good quantity of betelnuts from the King Shivaji.[138] Again in 1679, the British merchants procured more than two hundred Khandies of betelnuts at Rajapur.[139] Apart from these products, opium produced in the territory adjoining to Cheul was of enough circulation in other markets. Turmeric was produced on considerable scale and was exported to other territories.

Shivaji's Trade Control of Agrarian Goods

The present discussion aims to throw a light on how Shivaji tried to control over trade and also the prices of essential goods in his country, for the welfare of his people.

From the contemporary records it appears that the foreign travellers or traders required the passports for coming to the Maratha country or travelling through the territories of Shivaji's State. The Dutch record mentions that no one could pass through the country without a pass to be secured from Shivaji's officers.[140]

The trading ships belonging to foreign merchants had to obtain a permit from the Maratha government without which they could not enter harbour. Hence, the English merchants and others had secured the permit from Shivaji's officer at Kalyan Bhivandi for conducting their trade of different commodities at these places.[141] The goods of foreign merchants that came to Shivaji ports like Rajapur, Cheul, Dabhol, Kalyan or in any part of his dominions were valued at the custom house and the traders *had to pay the custom duty at the rate of* $2\frac{1}{2}$ *per cent on import or export goods.*[142] The English factors at Bombay paid custom dues to Shivaji for the goods like timber they purchased from his territories.[143]

If the foreign ships loaded with merchandise entered the ports or sailed in his seas without securing the permit from the Maratha government were confiscated by Shivaji's officers. For example, in 1677, when the Portuguese four ships loaded with wheat, gram and other foodgrains and sailing from Cambay to Goa, were seized by the Maratha officer at Rajapur, because the ships entered the port of Rajapur without securing the passports from the Maratha Government.[144] Likewise, in 1679 when the Portuguese cargoship laden with goods coming from Cambay took shelter in one of the river ports of Shivaji (Zangizara river or Sangmeshwar river) the subhedar of his port confiscated the ships and refused to release them without securing the permit from the Maratha King, Shivaji.[145] The State under Shivaji controlled the export trade of foodgrains and timber during the period of hostility. Thus, the export trade of timber and foodstuffs were forbidden by Shivaji during the years 1670[146] and 1674[147] respectively. The King restricted the export of timber to Bombay because, he was aware of the fact that the English were one of his competitors on the sea water. His purpose behind the prohibition of the export of grains to Bombay was political. He prohibited the export of rice from his country to the English at Bombay because the latter had good relations with the Siddhis, the enemy of Shivaji. Moreover the English had rendered the help to the Siddhis against the Maratha King.

Shivaji held the control over the import trade also. He restricted the import of salt of Bardez by imposing heavy duties on it.[148] The intention of Shivaji for imposing the high duty on import trade seems to be obvious. He wanted to protect the home industry of salt making against the Portuguese competition and sell the local salt cheaper than imported one.

In 1677, Shivaji made a blockade of the trade of clothes, rice and such other necessaries, which previously came from Cambay, passing through the Maratha territories to Goa. The blockade of the Portuguese trade was the result of the wars of Shivaji which broke out with the Adilshah and the ruler of Karnataka. As a result, all the supplies to be taken from Cambay to Goa, while passing through his country, were stopped by Shivaji. The blockade was so successful that it could not provide the commodities or foodgrains to Portuguese who suffered great loss and faced the serious problem of scarcity of foodgrains in their territories.[149] Shivaji also stopped the trade carried on a road from Balaghat, connecting the inland markets and linking Nagothane Bombay and to the sea coast when the hostility with the English arose (1674). He also ordered his officers to prohibit the commodities or goods being sent from Bombay to his territories.[150] The prohibition of intercourse with his enemy is an important aspect of, Shivaji's trade policy. And this policy of Shivaji must not be misinterpreted. The notable thing is that Shivaji applied the prohibition of intercourse only to his enemy territories. Secondly, this aspect of trade policy was not only applied by Shivaji alone. As contemporary records reveal it was also followed by the Portuguese. The Portuguese had prohibited all the supplies to be sent from Karnataka to Bombay through their territories, when the English supplied the foodgrains to the Arabs, their enemy, in times of hostility.[151] Again, due to their hostility with the Dutch, the Portuguese prohibited their trade with Shivaji's country and captured some trading vessels of Shivaji which traded with the ports belonging to the Dutch.[152] Thus, it seems that the prohibition of trade was the practice followed by the medieval Indian rulers as well as by the foreigners to settle their disputes. And it is the well known fact that the prohibition was in force only for a few years and was removed as soon as the hostility came to an end. Smuggling the goods from other territories to Shivaji's province was subject to severe punishment to the traders. Thus, when a smuggler, Sewalal Marwadi smuggled the goods, gold and silver coins from Goa to the city of Dicholi which was under the jurisdiction of Maratha King was caught by Shivaji's guards and kept at the border. From the advice of the Portuguese viceroy of Goa, it seems that the officer of Shivaji had confiscated all the goods, gold and silver coins smuggled by the smuggler.[153]

Like other rulers, Shivaji also undertook different measures for controlling agricultural prices. In order to maintain the supply of foodgrains in the markets and to check their rising prices during the days of scarcity, he imported rice from the places like Karwar,[154] Karnataka,[155] Goa,[156] Barselore,[157] etc. Sometimes, his officers at the ports allowed the ships loaded with foodstuffs to enter the ports by levying tariff only at half the usual rates. It was so when the scarcity arose in 1677 which was the result of the prohibition of trade between Maratha country and Portuguese territories. The restriction on trade was due to the hostility between Shivaji and the Portuguese.

Therefore during this year when many ships loaded with foodgrains belonging to native traders came at Cheul, the officer of Shivaji allowed the ships to enter the port by levying octroi duty on goods only according to the wish of traders i.e.

only half of the usual custom rate.[158] Thus, the importation of foodgrains by levying half octroi duty certainly served the aim though not lowering their prices, but of preventing food prices from rising high up and also regulating the volume of trade. Shivaji had his own stores. Each of his forts had the store where the foodgrains were stocked.[159] The grain stocked in Government store houses was released into the markets with a view to increase its supply in the market and prevent food prices from going high up during the period of scarcity. Thus, the supply of goods from the Government stores to the markets served as a good system for keeping the food prices stable.

Again as long as there are no big number of competitors or merchants in the trade, the prices do not rise and a few merchants fully exploit the situation by demanding the goods at low prices from the peasants. Hence Shivaji encouraged the free competition in trade in the market. Thus, in 1671, Shivaji made an agreement with the traders of Burhanpur and other parts that while passing through his territories, they should pay him only one rupee as a tax to be collected from their goods (bullock load).

Shivaji's permission for free passage to the traders naturally resulted in increase in number of merchants at Hubly and ultimately encouraged the free competition among the traders who specialised in the trade of barkley[160] (mire).

Thus, Shivaji's policy of trade control of agricultural goods, certainly benefited the consumers or common men who paid a reasonable price for goods they purchased. Likewise, his policy or the measures like reducing the rate of custom duty encouraged the free trade competition among the traders and proved beneficial to the producers because they could sell their goods at high prices which they expected.

References and Footnotes

1. Among the recent studies, Justice M.G. Ranade's Rise of Maratha Power, Bombay, 1900, and S.K Krishnaswami Aiyangar, "The Rise of the Maratha Power in the South," *Journal of Indian History*, Vol. IX, Parts I to III, 1930 and Shivaji and the Rise of Maharattas, by Richard Temples and others, need special mention.
2. N.K. Behere, The Background of Maratha Renaissance in the 17th century, 1946.
3. Satish Chandra, "Social Background to the Rise of the Maratha Movement during the 17th Century in India", *The Indian Economic and Social History Review*, X, 3, Sept. 1973, pp. 209-217.
4. Marathanchya Itihasachi Sadhane, V.K. Rajwade, Vol. No. I, Aitihasik Prastavana, p 258. Also see Maharashtrachya Jivanatil Sthityantare, by B.S. Pandit, Poona University Publication, 1968, p. 66.
5. Ibid. It is obvious from the example of a Hindu person namely Srikhande who lost his life in fighting with the Muslims for the Watan, but he did not leave his claim for the same Watan.
6. Ghauri, I.A., "Central Structure of the Kingdom of Bijapur", *Islamic Culture*, XLIV, No 1, 1970, p. 28.
7. Bendre, V.S , Qutubshahi of Golkonda in the 17th century, 1934, p. 67.
8. Bharat Itihas Sanshodhaka Mandal Quarterly, (B.I.S.M.), June 1922, and Shejwalkar's Chhatrapati Shivaji, p. 491.
9. Cambridge History of India, Vol. III, p. 485.
10. Mirat-I-Ahmadi, Vol. I, p 265. Also see History of India as told by its own Historians, by Elliot and Dowson, Vol. VII, p. 293.
11. Peter Floris, "His Voyage to the East Indies, 1611-15 Ed. by W.H. Moreland, 1934, p. 14.
12. Ibid., p. 22.
13. *Islamic Culture*, Vol. LI, No. I, Jan. 1977, p. 60.
14. Shivkalin Patra Sar Sangrah, (SPSS) Vol. I, nos. 155, 1187,
15. Ibid., No 1192.
16. Lane Pool, Medieval India, p. 105.
17. Sherwani, H.K., and Joshi, P.M., History of Medieval Deccan, p. 399.

18. Verma, D.C., History of Bijapur, p. 245.

19. Parasnis, D.D., Musalmani Amaddnitil Maratha Sardars, 39-43; also see Rajwade's MIS, XX.

20. *Tarikh-I-Farista*, edited and translated by Briggs, 1908, Vol. I, 527.

21. B.I.S.M. Quarterly, Year 62, nos. 1-4, July 1983-Oct. 1983, p. 97.

22. Bharat Itihas Ani Sanskriti, Quarterly of Mumbai, Marathi Grantha Sangrahalaya, Jan. 1976, No. 48, p 68.

23. Moreland, W.H., India at the Death of Akbar, p. 274.

24. Ibid.

25. Linschoten, I, 260-63.

26. *Islamic Culture*, Vol. LI, No. 3, July 1977, p 197.

27. *Islamic Culture*, XLIV, No. I, Jan. 1970, p. 28.

28. Verma, D.C., op. cit., p. 233.

29. Elements of South Indian Palaegraphy, p. 112.

30. Grant Duff, "History of the Marathas", Vol. I p. 497.

31. Radheysham, "The Kingdom of Ahmednagar", p. 285.

32. Andre Wink, "The Settlement of the Deccan 1600-1680", *B.I.S.M.* Quarterly 60, 1-4, 1981, pp. 48 to 50.

33. Richards, J.R., Mughal Administration in Golkonda, 1975, p. 22.

34. Moreland, op. cit., pp. 135-136.

35. Verma, D.C., op. cit., p. 233.

36. Ghauri, I.A., "Local Government under the Sultanates of Bijapur and Golkonda-Haiderabad", *Islamic Culture*, Vol. LI, No. I, Jan. 1977, p. 56 and p. 64.

37. SPSS, I, letter No. 50.

38. Ibid.

39. Zakir Husain, "The Working of the Jagir System in the Deccan during the last years of Aurangzeb". Papers on *Indian History*, (Cyclostyled), presented by Aligarh Muslim University in 47th Session of IHC 1986, Srinagar, p. 42, The Document though belongs to the later period, it appears that the practice of illegal exaction seems to have been previously existed in Deccan since the regime of Muslim Sultans.

40. Selected Waqai Deccan, ed. Yusuf Hussain, Haiderabad, 1953, document-15, p. 18. *Islamic Culture*, Vol. LI, No. 1, Jan. 1977, p. 58.

41. SPSS, III, 2423.

42. Records of the Shivaji period, (RSP) (ed. by Khobrekar), letter No. 8.

43. Basatin-us-Salatin, the work translated into Marathi and published in *Shivacharitra Vritta Sangraha*, Vol. II, BISM publication 1939, No 52. Also see *Islamic Culture*, Vol. XLVI, No. 1, Jan. 1972, p. 51.

44. Zahiruddin Faruki, Aurangzeb and his Times, p. 154.

45. Ghauri, I. A., Kingship in the Sultanates of Bijapur and Golkonda, *Islamic Culture*, XLVI, No 1, Jan. 1972, p. 52.

46. *Islamic Culture*, XLIX, No. 4, Oct. 1975, p. 228.

47. Richards, J.F., op. cit., pp. 137, 138.

48. SPSS, III, No. 2367.

49. Manucci, II, 234; also see J.F. Richards, op. cit., p. 138.

50. Shivcharitra Sahitya (SCS), II, 173.

51. Ibid., II, 156.

52. *Islamic Culture*, Vol. XLIV, No. 1, Jan. 1970, p. 28; also see Sen's Administrative System of the Marathas, pp. 82-83.

53. For the details of the taxes relating to various subjects in Adilshahi kingdom under Muhammad Adilshah, Adilshah II, and Sikandar Adilshah, see A.R. Kulkarni, "Nilanga Parmane, Ek Abhyas", *Bhartiya Itihas Ani Sanskriti*, Vol. 4, No. 15, Oct. 1967, pp. 39-47; also see Ghauri, I.A., "Local Government under the Sultanates of Bijapur and Golkonda-Haiderabad," *Islamic Culture*, Vol. LI, No. I, Jan. 1977, p. 67.

54. It was a kind of Nazarpatti, to be paid by the rayat to the Sultan in a year. See Khobrekar, RSP, p. 5.

55. It was a tax levied on villages. From Mauje Baribayalin Poona Pargana under Nizamshahi rule 2½ hons were collected in a year; see RSP, by Khobrekar, p. 38.

56. Tamaskar, B.G., The life and work of Malik Ambar, p. 267.

57. *Islamic Culture*, XLIV, No. 1, 1970, p. 28.

58. Ghauri, I.A., in his article, "Local Government under Sultanates of Bijapur and Golkonda", in *Islamic Culture*, Vol. LI, No. 1, Jan. 1977, p. 67, has given the list of taxes collected from cultivators. They indicate the heavy burden of taxes imposed on the masses. It was a tax to be borne by the people to meet the expenses of the guests of the state.

59. Khobrekar, op. cit., p. 34.
60. From a small village like mauje Wade in Poona Pargana the tax was 20 takas and 50 takas from big village of Bhayewadi; see Khobrekar, op. cit., pp. 34-35.
61. Masir-I-Jahangiri, by Kwaja Kamgar Husaini, ed. by Azra Alavi, 1978, p. 333, quoted from the papers on Indian History (cyclostyled), presented by Aligarh Muslim University, 47th session of IHC, Srinagar, p. 141.
62. Iqbalnama-I-Jahangiri, Mutamadkhan, Nowalkishor, Lucknow, 1870, Vol. II, p. 592.
63. Gribble, J.D.B., A History of the Deccan, Vol. I, London, 1986, p. 249.
64. Elliot and Dowson, op. cit., Vol. VI, No. III, pp. 149-150.
65. *Ferista*, by Briggs, I, p. 167.
66. Sharma, S.R., The Founding of Maratha Freedom, p. 62.
67. *Tarikh-I-Ferista*, by Briggs, Vol. II, p. 293.
68. Ibid., II, 315.
69. Modak, B.P., A History of the Mahomedan Kingdoms in the Deccan, (1891). Vol III, p. 76.
70. Ibid., p. 161.
71. Elliot and Dowson, op. cit., Vol. VII, pp. 52-56.
72. Ibid., Vol. VII, p. 57.
73. SPSS, I, 332.
74. Ibid , 308, 328.
75. J.D.B. Gribble, op cit., Vol. I, pp. 194-195.
76. Joshi, P.M., "The Portuguese on the Deccan (Konkan) Coast, Sixteenth and Seventeenth Centuries", *Journal of Indian History*, Vol. XLVI, Part-I, April, 1968, No. 136, pp. 74-82.
77. Gupta, A.D., A Historical Note on Dabhol, forgotten port of Konkan, a paper (cyclostyled) presented at the U.G.C. Seminar on Konkan Society held at Poona University, Pune, October, 1984.
78. Tamaskar, B.G., op. cit., p. 345.
79. *Journal of Indian History*, IX, Part-I and III, 1930, p. 188 (footnote).
80. SPSS, III, 2478.
81. Shiva Bharat Canto 8, 53-55.
82. Ibid., Canto 8, 52.

83. Nayeem, M.A., "New Light on Mughal Jagirdari System," *Islamic Culture*, Vol. LIV, No. 2, April 1980, p. 95. The article pertains to the period 1653-58 of the provinces in Deccan under the Vice Royalty of Aurangzeb. The author in the background considerably sheds light on declined income of land revenue and financially weak position of Deccan subas including Daulatabad, Berar and Ahmednagar after 1636.
84. Zakir Husain, op. cit., p. 42
85. *Islamic Culture*, XLIV, No. 1, 1970, p. 28.
86. SPSS, I, letter No. 50.
87. Verma, D.C , op. cit., p. 235.
88. Peter Floris, op. cit., p. 22.
89. SPSS, III, 2525.
90. Kulaba Gazetteer, p. 285.
91. SPSS, III, letter No. 2687. The record shows that 1/4 taka was imposed on each loom, in Bijapur kingdom under Ali Adilshah II. A wool dealer paid 5 pounds of wool per loom and one blanket per loom from a weaver; see Peshwa Daftar, XXXI, 55.
92. Kulaba Gazetteer, p. 285.
93. Ibid.
94. Itihas Ani Sanskriti Maharashtra Rajya Sahitya Mandal Quarterly, Jan. 1976, No. 48, pp. 67-68.
95. Ibid.
96. Sharma, R.S., op. cit , p. 146.
97. *Islamic Culture*, LI, No. 1, Jan. 1977, p. 67.
98. *Ferista*, II, by Briggs, p. 21.
99. SCS, IX, p. 65.
100. Sherwani, H.K. and Joshi, P.M., op. cit., p. 405.
101. SPSS, I, 482.
102. Ibid., I, 482.
103. Ibid., III, 2466.
104. Asraf, K.M., Life and Conditions of the People of Hindustan, p. 140.
105. SPSS, I, 329.
106. Ibid., 313.
107. Ibid., III, 2379.
108. Here the prices of necessaries in the kingdom of Golkonda are taken into consideration. It is possible that except the famine period those prices would not have been very different than those prevailing in the Adilshahi and Nizamshahi kingdoms.

109. One maund was equal to 40 seers of those days.
110. Sherwani, H.K and Joshi, P.M., op. cit., p. 475.
111. Sambhajikalin Patrasar Sangrah, B.I.S.M., Quarterly series No. 75, letter No. 32.
112. Sherwani, H K. and Joshi, P.M., op. cit., p. 475.
113. Shiva Charitra Pradeep, p. 109.
114. Moreland, op. cit., p. 269.
115. Asraf, K.M., op. cit., p. 291.
116. Sherwani, H.K. and Joshi, P.M., op. cit., p. 405.
117. Rajwade, V.K., op. cit., Vol. VIII, letter No. 28. It is obvious from an order which Shivaji issued in 1673 to his soldiers forbidding them from damaging the crops of peasants and also prohibiting them from taking away forcefully the grains, vegetables etc. from the cultivators.
118. Ibid. The same document contains strict warnings given to soldiers by Shivaji for not molesting the civil population and to be vigilant, lest the people would say you are not better than the Mughals.
119. Ibid.
120. SCS IX, 55.
121. Ibid , V, 996.
122. Rajwade, V.K., op. cit., Vol. XV, 276, SPSS, III, 2466.
123. Mahaley, K.L., "Shivaji the Pragmatist", 1969, p. 58.
124. ERS, II, p. 2.
125. Tavernier, J.B., Travels in India, Vol. II, p. 11.
126. ERS, Part II, pp. 324-25.
127. ERS, Part-I, 384.
128. Jean Baptiste Tavernier, op. cit., Vol. II, p. 11.
129. ERS, I, 382, p. 277.
130. Ibid. II, 284.
131. Ibid., II, 24.
132. Ibid., II, p. 108.
133. Ibid., II, 2, p. 2.
134. Ibid., II, 103.
135. Ibid., II, 207.
136. Ibid., II, 377, p. 206.
137. Ibid., II, 165.
138. Ibid., II, 207.
139. Ibid., II, p. 152.

140. FBS, ed. by Sen p. 211.
141. SPSS, Vol. I, letter No. 1310.
142. ERS, I, 473, pp. 348-49.
143. SPSS, I, letter No. 1310.
144. Shivshahi Portuguese Kagadpatre (edited by S.S. Desai), letter No. 44.
145. Ibid., letter No. 66.
146. SPSS, I, letter No. 1633.
147. ERS, I, 227.
148. SPSS, II, letter No. 1430.
149. Shivshahi Portuguese Kagadpatre, letter No. 40.
150. SPSS, II, letter No. 1642.
151. Ibid., II, letter No. 2088.
152. Ibid., II, letter No. 2082.
153. Shivshahi Portuguese Kagadpatre, letter No. 82.
154. ERS I, 164.
155. Shivshahi Portuguese Kagadpatre, letter No. 69.
156. Ibid., letter No. 63.
157. Ibid., letter No. 62.
158. SPSS, II, 1908.
159. Ibid., II, 1909, p. 568.
160. ERS, I, 261, p. 191.

2

Land, Land Rights and Peasantry in Maratha Kingdom

The agrarian history of any state involves the topics such as the types of land, land revenue, land tenure, land rights, agricultural crops and implements, agro-technology, life of peasants, the relationship between the class of peasantry and tenants, landed aristocracy, noblemen, ruling class etc. It also includes the study of the agrarian conditions, the land taxes, burden of taxation, the exploitation of peasantry by the landlords, money lenders and the government officers, the peasants' reaction to it, the measures undertaken by the rulers for the upliftment of peasantry. The following discussion is a focus upon some of the above mentioned aspects of the agrarian history of the society in Maharashtra under Shivaji.

Land System

In the contemporary records relating to the land revenue, we find following various terms used for productive as well as for unproductive land. Those terms clearly reveal the importance of the quality of soil, meaning of the land provided with water supply, suitability of land for sowing various types of crops etc. The study of those records shows distinguished terms like Samin[1] land (superior land), Katuban[2] and Kudthal[3] (fallen land or barren land), Kuran[4] or grass land.

The term 'Kudthal' or 'Katuban' can be interpreted as barren land. The record pertaining to Poona Pargana of the year 1653-54 mentions that the villages like mauje Hadpsar, Vanvadi etc., had some barren lands and therefore those lands were exempted from the payment of revenue.[5]

There are other terms mentioned in our sources of the royal period for the land brought under cultivation. With a view to consider the sources of water supply the cultivable tract was classified into following three types of land:

(i) Jirayat[6] (dry)
(ii) Bagayat[7] (wet)
(iii) Nipani[8] bagayat (not sufficient wet land).

Jirayat land was dependent on rain only. The second type of land was cultivated on water supply from the well and the river.[9] The term 'Khalati' indicates the tract that was suitable for growing the crop of rice. Nipani bagayat would mean the land that was not under sufficient water.

The terms like Charoom Raupal, Kharwut Bawul Khuree, Kueyat, Ruho Toorwut, Katahnee Manut etc., may mean rice lands.[10]

The land revenue record of mauje Bahuli in prant of Mawal also mentions the fields in which sugarcane could be sown on considerable scale. The terms such as Bardi[11] or hilly land, Talwat[12] (the tract near the foot of hills) etc., indicate the inferior but cultivable land. But the terms like Gavran[13] Gavthan, Padhargan,[14] Pandhari[15] etc., explain the tracts of village as untilled land which were used for habitation. The term Bedland[16] indicates the meaning of moisture tract. The land called as Pandhari, Gavthan etc., were no doubt the part of the land of village.

Villages in Poona pargana were recorded with pandhari land that was habitable.[17] The land revenue records of the village Bahuli also mention some other type of land. Those terms[18] are as given below:

(i) Awal (Superior)

(ii) Dum (Ordinary)

(iii) Sim (Inferior).

Those terms suggest that the lands were also classified on the quality or on the fertility. There were two types of bagayat land. Most of the land records refer to the terms 'Patsthal'[19] and Motsthal.[20] Patsthal means the land irrigated by canal water. The term Motsthal occurring in the documents of Shivaji's period can be explained as land irrigated by well water. The barren type of land is generally known as "Nikhar".[21] The villages like Menoli and others had such type of lands.

Some other terms have been mentioned in the records of Shivaji's period for the non-cultivable types of land.

The terms can be noted as follows:

1. Padit[22] (lying fallow or uncultivated)
2. Khadakmal[23] (rocky land)
3. Gayaran land (an open pasture ground applied for uncultivable land).

The term Kasland[24] occurring in our sources can be explained as the division of Khachari (rice land).

In some of our records the term Sheriland[25] has been found. Molesworth has explained the term Sheriland as garden ground or arable land which had never been included within the bonds of any village and which was held by the government. The king also donated such land to individuals as Inam land.

In the villages of Sayatan and Varasgaon in Poona Pargana, the Sheri lands granted as Inam to Gondaji Pasalkar Desai were one hundred bighas and eighty bighas respectively.

Inam Lands

The lands known as Inamati of the village were assigned to the Inamdars. Syed Adam Karim Sarja was granted some lands in the village of Sogur as Inam by the son of Shivaji for his military services to the State.[26] A large number of our records refer to the fact that the land revenue of some tracts of lands were assigned by the Maratha King to religious institutions like temples, mathas, mosques, or the tombs of the saints.

The revenue of those lands were granted for the maintenance of the worship of those religious places. Such Inamlands were called as Devsthan or Dharmadaya Inam.[27] The temple of saint Dhyaneshwar,[28] the mathas of Ramdas[29] and Mauni Bava[30] of Patgaon were granted such inams by the King Shivaji.

Inam Land Agrahar: Many grants of land of Shivaji's period refer to the Agrahar inamland. Thus, the land of the village Nadoli in Karhad Prant was Agrahar inam granted to Malhar Gosavi[31] by the King Shivaji.

Khalisa Land: The term Khalisa is taken to mean the land whose land revenue was despatched to the treasury of the State.

Peasant's Land Rights

The chief resource of the life of the agrarian classes in Maratha kingdom was the land. The possession of land which was considered as property was one of the predominant factors that could determine the social and political status of men in society. The land ownership has got its own significance from all points of view. Here, the aim of our discussion is to explain the nature of land control, the rights of ownership and possession in Maratha kingdom of the 17th century.

It is beyond doubt that all the land in the Maratha State belonged to the ruler.

Royal Ownership of Land

The records concerning the revenue of our period, the word 'Peshaji'[33] occurs for the ownership of the King. The King Shivaji, therefore, held complete control over the land in the Swaraj. But we have a number of evidences in those records which would show that other persons, government officers, Mirasdars, Watandars and peasants etc., also enjoyed the proprietary rights in land.

A grant of land made by the ruler of earlier dynasty was continued by the successive ruler of other dynasty. Thus, Naro Vishwanath,[34] a Kulkarni of Wai Pargana who was granted an inam land of half chavar by Adilshah II, also enjoyed the right in some land alongwith his other perquisites in the reign of King Shivaji. It is equally true that the Maratha King also possessed the power to set aside the land rights of an ordinary person whose ancestors enjoyed the land for centuries together with in favour of a scholar who secured higher merit. For instance, a grant of quarter chavar of land belonging to a shepherd was made by the ruler in favour of a Brahmin learned scholar.[35] The shepherd was then deprived of his right in land alongwith his other rights in garden and a well in the same tract.

This indicates that the ruler could transfer not only the rights in land but also other forms of property.

The watan system in medieval Maharashtra led to the emergence of the class of watandars or feudatories who enjoyed the rights over the land. The rights of lands of landed feudal class certainly contributed to the curtailment of the royal rights in land. The King being the master of the watandars had supreme power over the land, villages and provinces. Thus, the right of royal ownership over the land was superior to the right of the watandars who occupied inferior status in the eyes of common men.

Individual Ownership of Land

The possession of land by the individual would afford him the proprietary right in land. The possession of the field would acquire validity when the person received an agreement regarding the right in land (Khurdakhat) from the King. Bhikaji Bin Suryaji Dimale of mauje Siware in Khedbare pargana was granted twelve bighas of land by the King Shivaji for his services as a village Mokadam. The land which belonged to the Mokadam became valid or it got the legal basis when the King issued him a royal letter regarding his right over land called as 'Khurdakhat'. But the same Mokadam when failed in cultivating his land and left his village for some years, he was deprived of his right in land. This would mean that the individuals or the Mokadams had been in possession of lands which they brought under cultivation. Their ownership over the land was restricted only to the cultivation of the land in their possession. In this case, the reason mentioned in the record as to why the Mukadam was deprived of his right in land is certainly the non-cultivation of the land granted to the person by the King. Thus, it appears that the Maratha ruler could establish the royal ownership over the land of individuals by confiscating the uncultivated land from them.

It is interesting to note that when the land was granted to the donee all the rights over waters, trees, etc., were also transferred to him by the ruler. A grant of fifteen bighas of land was transferred to the Kazi of Wai and Kudal Pargana by the State.[37] The record further informs us that the rights in land were transferred to the donee alongwith other rights to mango and other fruit trees, waters etc.

The officials of King Shivaji were assigned part of revenue collected from the villages as the remuneration of their services to the State. For instance, a Mokadam of mauje Siware was remunerated by assigning to him some share of revenue as well as the inamland of twelve bighas of mauje Kalyan.[38] The practice of providing the grant of lands to the village officials that prevailed in medieval Maharashtra created not only a hereditary right in land but also led them to emerge as the landlords. It undoubtedly created the rights of their ownership over the land and raised their power and prestige in society.

It seems that the King Shivaji had granted the class of peasant proprietors the rights of ownership like sale and purchase or mortgage of the land. The study of land right in medieval Maharashtra can be demonstrated by discussing some examples of all rights of ownership of the land of individuals. Anto Krishna had sold his land to Abdul Kadar at Newase for five hons.[39] Timaji Namaji Kulkarni at Loni had purchased the watan land by paying forty-five hons to the seller.[40] Similarly, a peasant in pargana Kudal sold out his fifteen bighas of land to Naik Deshmukh of that pargana.[41]

Due to famine condition a Mirasdar namely Kumaji in Junnar pargana, had to sell his ten bighas of land for one hundred fifty hons to Abaji Sondev, alongwith his rights of Kulkarni and Joshi watan of mauje Tandali in tarf Rajangaon.[42] Kechangauda Patil at mauje Savasi in prant of Bhujbalgad gave up his right of ownership over ten bighas of lands by taking one hundred fifty hons from Narsingrau Ramaji.[43]

Above cited instances indicate that the group of bigger land owners including in it the village watandars and money lenders in Maratha kingdom purchased the lands from small peasants by offering them low prices. The sale of the land belonging to the small peasant proprietors not only contributed to decrease their land rights but also reduced them to poorer tenants. On the contrary, such practice could help the land owners to convert themselves into a class of bigger landlords or Zamindars. This again resulted in the increase in the number of dependent peasants losing their land rights as well as social status in the society.

Collective Land Rights

The instances of the concept of collective rights in land in Maratha kingdom under Shivaji can be found in our contemporary records. The terms used for collective rights of village people in land are such as Gayaran[44] (land for grazing the cows or cattle), Gavthal, Gavthan or village site etc. The grass land on the bank of river or pasture fields may be considered as uncultivated land over which the inhabitants of the village had common rights. It seems that the village population of mauje Baje[45] of peth Hukeri had collective right over the uncultivated land of the pasture fields where the cattle could graze. One hundred twenty-one bighas of lands of the villages of Shahapur, Risawad, Umbraj-Sirgaon, Vadigaon etc. were granted to the temple of the Math of Ramdas at Chaphal.[46] As the god in the temple was worshipped by all the people, the land donated to such math belonged to all the communities.

The evidence of collective rights over the village land in parganas like Poona and others can be found in granting the lands to the temples of gods like Ganapati.[47]

The effort of planting of the fruit trees and flower plants is a good example of common property rights of different communities. Likewise, the rights over the grass lands of the villages like Veharvade[48] and also over the pasture fields on the banks of the rivers in Poona pargana, could be enjoyed by the inhabitants of the villages for the purpose of grazing of the cattle. The land at all sides of the village was left uncultivated. Such land was used by the rural folk for their common purposes. The inhabitants of the village Khor in taluka Karhe-Pathar had tracts of uncultivable land called as Thalland, jungle land.[49] Over these tracts demonstrating the boundary of the mauje, all the people enjoyed their rights.

Another evidence of the community rights over the land that can be given and found in our sources is the land granted by the government to Muslim inhabitants of the village for erecting the Darga on such land or for burying of the dead bodies of the Muslim people in the land.[50]

The instances cited above regarding the land rights show that the individual property rights in land and communal property rights also existed in Maratha kingdom of the seventeenth century.

Demarcation of the Boundaries of Land

It is found that the boundaries of the Inamlands granted by the Maratha King to the individuals or to the Mathas of the saints were also mentioned in concerning records. For instance, the Mirasi land granted to Ramaji Vithal Deshkulkarni has been found demarcated as given below:

"The land attached to the village was one chavar where a huge fig tree grew near the stream called as Nagzari." Some of the lands were brought under the cultivation of cocoanut trees near the dry well.[51] The boundaries of other lands were demarcated by the temple. Thus, the boundary of the land of four chavar granted as Inamland in mauje Chambali and Narayanpur in taluka Karhepathar to Manaji Shankar[52] Nilkanthrao was demarcated by the temples situated near the Pandhar land etc. i.e. the boundaries of the village. The mango trees also found mentioned in those lands. Very often, the boundaries of the lands were mentioned near the wall of the palace or near the land where plenty of Bel trees grew.[53]

The type of Inamland also seems to have been mentioned in those records. Thus, the Inamland of half chavar and twenty bighas granted to Jayaram Bhat of Kasba Wai has been clearly demarcated as irrigated land attached to mauje Sihali near Koregaon and the boundary of big Nhavi village.[54]

One-quarter chavar of land granted as Inamland to Naro Vishwanath Pandit was clearly demarcated by mentioning that the tract of Kasbe Nauraspur belonging to Mir Dhangar and lying near the wall of town, was the garden land and some portion of it was the barren trip.[55]

Peasants in Maratha Kingdom

Agrarian class in Maharashtra under Shivaji was consisted of the following groups:

(i) The proprietors called as Mirasdars or Thalkaris.

(ii) Kunbis and Upris were the tenant cultivators.

(iii) The hereditary village officials such as Patil, Deshmukh, Kulkarni, Deshpande etc, who acted as intermediaries between the government and the peasants.

Terms for Peasants

While studying the contemporary records of our period, we come across the various terms for the class of peasants. The term 'thalkari' has been used for a cultivator. The word 'Mirasdars'[56] is used for the cultivaters who possessed their own land. The terms 'Upris',[57] 'Kunbis',[58] 'Kultrs etc.'[59] have been used for the tenant cultivators who tilled the lands belonging to others.

Mirasdar: Mirasdar was the peasant born in low or high caste family and held the land in the village. The men born in the families of the castes like Brahmin, Washerman, Shepherd[60] and Patil and such others possessing the hereditary claims over the land were called as Mirasdar. Though the land belonged to the Mirasdar and his family, the rights over the land could be given up by selling it to others. The mirasdar had also his permanent house in the village. Thus, a mirasdar belonging to Brahmin caste, namely Kumaji Joshi who lived in the village of Tandali in tarf Ranjangaon possessed a mirasi land of ten bighas. But he gave up his rights over the land by selling the land and house to other person namely Abaji Sondev.[61] Such lands held by a particular family could be separated from the land granted to it as Inam land by the

King. The tenant who purchased the Mirasi land from the mirasdar could thus enjoy the rights over the land by becoming the Mirasdar in the village.[62]

Kunbis and Upris

The feudal characteristics can also be found in Maratha kingdom during the 17th century. We find numerous instances of making grants of lands or villages to the Brahmanas or other persons. The King Shivaji also continued the practice of making grants of rent free lands to the village watandars or the balutedars.[63] This practice was also carried on by the successors of Shivaji. This type of process led to the emergence and growth of the lower peasants or tenant cultivators in medieval Maharashtra. The word Upris cultivated the land belonging to others and did not possess the permanent land. The lands of watandars and such others were rented out to such peasants. The Goverment hereditary officials, Brahmanas or other landholders got their land cultivated by temporary peasants.

The term 'Kunbawa' occurring very rarely in our records may be noted as the indication of the agricultural work performed by the peasant called as Kunbi. Such cultivator who held the land as perpetual estate under acknowledgement had to pay certain rent or the land tax to the Government.[64] The Kunbawa could also secure social status as a watandar when the former purchased the watan from the latter. Thus, Balaji Patil of mauje Khadale held one chavar of land as perpetual estate. But he purchased the Patilki watan of the village from the village Patil and also secured the right of watan from the Government[65] and consequently he raised his social status by becoming the village watandar.

The term Mirasdar Kunbi is used to those who possessed the right in the land. Thus, Sivji Patil and Mankoji Bhos of mauje Tadali in Taluka Ranjangaon in prant of Junnard., sold their mirasi watan, ten bighas of irrigated land to the Mirasdar Kunbi of the village.[66] The record clearly mentions that by transferring the land of the mirasdar to the Mirasi Kunbis, the latter could be converted into Mirasi or Mirasdar who had hereditary rights in land. This shows that the Mirasi Kunbi were also the cultivators. Though they did not possess permanent claim over the land, but they cultivated the land leased to them. Narsoji Naikada[67] was a Kunbi of mauje Shirade and he tilled the land of the Zamindar in the Umbaraj Pargana.

It appears that among the temporary peasants who were large in number than those of the Zamindars and watandars, the 'rayat kul'[68] were very common. It is to be noted here that the word Kul or 'rayat kul' found in our records is used to mean usually the group of peasants who cultivated the land of Zamindars, Watandars and they were the tenants.

Sometimes the tenants left the villages and migrated to other places. As a result, the fields of land owners remained uncultivated.[69] The tenants in mahal Thane left their villages and migrated to other localities in 1689-90 A.D. Therefore, the Government officials encouraged them to come to their native places and gave them exemptions in the taxes that were levied upon them.[70]

Similarly, some temporary peasants were brought by the officers from other villages to cultivate the land in village Borghar in Cheul prant. It shows that some tenants were employed for tilling the government land for a temporary period. Such peasants rented the lands of the watandars or the fields of the State. Other records[71] reveal that the migration of temporary peasants took place to other villages when the provision for their food and houses were made by the land owners.

The king Shivaji who encouraged the temporary peasants for making them permanent cultivators, thus, played a vital role in creating new class of the peasants. Such cultivators were based on the grants of lands for digging wells in the fields or constructing the canals for irrigation etc. For instance, Chatoji Ramaji and Kanhoji Shivaji, two brothers of mauje Rahatwade in tarf Karhepathar were granted the inamland by the State because they constructed a well in the tract of land for irrigating the soil.[72] Likewise, a person who built a lake was awarded the prize of inamland.[73] These examples reveal that the persons who were only tenants and cultivated the land of others, could also become the permanent peasants who possessed the right over their land.

The tenants or temporary peasants who could obtain the status of a mirasdar by digging wells on the lands belonging to the State on which they worked as temporary peasants, were also holding the responsibility of the payment of revenue tax.

Factors Responsible for Deteriorating the Position of the Peasants

Political and economic factors which hampered the economic growth of the State, consequently led to deteriorating conditions of the peasantry in Maratha kingdom in the seventeenth century.

Among the political forces Shivaji's struggles with his enemies like the Mughals, the Siddhis, the Adilshah, the Portuguese, and his military expeditions against the foes, the marching of the enemy's army through the territories of his kingdom etc., struck the heavy blow on the agricultural economy of the Maratha State. The plunders of peasants' property by the troops of enemy again worsened the economic condition of the ploughmen.

Some other factors discussed below, also weakened the position of peasantry in medieval Maharashtra.

Natural Calamities

The famines, floods, droughts etc., were sources of destruction of the economic prosperity of the peasantry.

The description of the distressed condition of peasantry in Maratha State has been found in the contemporary records of our period. A detailed information of the famines occurred in Maratha country, has been given in the present study elsewhere. During the famine period, a large number of people died because of starvation[74] and hunger. This also resulted in depopulating of many villages in the kingdom.[75] Many peasants sold their lands, watan, ploughs, bullocks, houses due to the heavy indebtedness.[76] Thus, the starvation, sufferings and misery etc., were the notable features of the life of peasants in Maratha kingdom during the famine period. Among the natural calamities which caused misery to the peasants, the natural diseases like 'Mehu' or 'Tambara'[76A] may be mentioned. Marathi documents, pertaining to the seventeenth century, refer to the 'Mehu' widespread disease in the provinces of the kingdom. The kharif and rabi crops of mauje Sekhapur[77] in prant of Man, though could not become the victim of this disease, but the same disease widely spreading over agricultural crops in other provinces, must have destroyed the produce and brought the distressing conditions to the peasants. Such type of natural diseases destroying the agricultural crops had become a common phenomenon of rural life during the medieval period of Maharashtra.

Plunders of Peasant's Property by the Enemy's Army

Another factor that led to the declining condition of peasantry was the plunder of their property by the army of an enemy. The troops of foes plundered their houses, food-grains, bullocks, etc.

In 1684 A.D., the troops of the Portuguese plundered three villages in mamale Cheul and carried away all the agricultural produce from them.[78] The same region was again plundered by the enemy in 1687 A.D. The plunder also resulted in depopulating of many towns and villages.[79] In 1685 A.D., the Mughal army plundered not only the houses of the peasants, but also looted the market places[80] in the province. The plunder of their wealth and property also resulted in making peasants the land labourers.

Oppression by Government Officials

Oppression by government officers is one of the important causes of the misery of the peasant classes. The village officers, the havaldars, Jumaledars, clerks etc., caused sufferings to the poor farmers by harassing them. They exploited the peasants by extracting more than what was due from them. The harassment of the peasants by the officers in form of Vethbigar also compelled them to take plight to other region.[81] The condition of the peasants was again worsened when the officers took forcibly the foodgrains, vegetables and other necessary articles from them. This type of harassment of the peasantry by government officials became the matter of worry and serious consideration for the king who strictly warned them and prohibited them, from doing so by issuing the royal orders.[82] The government officers in town engaged some peasants as hired labourers on private works. But those peasants were not paid for their work. The officials, thus, imposed forced labour upon them.[83]

Vethbegar (forced labour)

The practice of employing the forced labour also worsened the economic condition of peasantry of our period. The peasants were engaged in agricultural work as unpaid forced labour. The Watandars or the government officials imposed forced labour on cultivators for their own private work as well as for the services of the villages. They were also employed as agricultural labourers on state farms. The government demanded free services from them for cultivating the state land or for manuring and irrigating the fields.[84] The task of doing a hedge of thorns in surroundings of the crop fields was to be performed by the peasants. They were engaged in the works of cutting of the grass from the grass land, or cutting of woods or trees from the forest etc. The forced labour compelled many peasants to abandon their villages. Consequently, they took shelter to other localities.

The migration of the cultivators resulted in remaining their lands uncultivated. As a result, the peasants who lost the agricultural produce, became the victims of hunger and poverty.[85]

Heavy Taxes

The King Shivaji provided protection to his rayats in exchange of collection of the cesses from them. Various taxes imposed on them enhanced miserable condition of peasantry. The land revenue was the main source of the income of the State, so the King collected land tax from peasants. Usually two-fifth or one-half share of the total produce was collected as State demand from the cultivators by the King.[86]

In contemporary records, we come across different kinds of taxes which were realised by the King. Prof. A.R. Kulkarni has discussed in detail various taxes imposed on the people in Maratha kingdom by Shivaji.[87] We may have a long list of taxes such as Miraspatti[88], Inampatti[89], Sinhasanpatti[90], Sadilwar Patti, house tax, Tutpatti, Gavkharchapatti. In addition to these, many other taxes imposed upon peasantry, included the levies like Jangampatti, Dasarapatti[91], Mejwanipatti[92], Thanpatti[93],Toranpatti, gavtake etc. A list of numerous taxes indicate that the King imposed considerable burden of taxes upon the peasantry who had provided the largest share of the revenue to the State.

How the Peasants Reacted to Heavy Taxation?

The exploitation of peasantry by the government officials or watandars created discontent among them. The peasants expressed their discontent against the oppressive taxes by leaving their native locality where such levies were covered. They took plights to other region where no such tax was imposed upon them.

The Deshmukh and Desak of Wai Pargana imposed exhorbitant taxes on peasants. As a result of which, the rayat left that pargana and migrated to other territories.[94] The peasants abandoned their villages and migrated to other places in order to escape from the burden of illegal taxes imposed upon them by the government officials. In our records, we find ample evidences of peasants' desertion which took place from time to time. Those references throw a considerable light on how the farmers reacted to the oppressive taxes by expressing their discontentment in form of mass desertion.

Peasant's protest against over-taxation can also be seen in the complaints made by the landholders to the King against the government officers. For instance, a hereditary Inam land holder namely Niloji Nilkanthrao of mauje Chambali in prant of Poona, made the complaint againt Ragho Bhaskar who imposed twenty-five hons as miraspatti upon the said Inamdar.[95] In fact as per agreement this tax was not to be levied and not to be collected from the mirasis holding lands in Pune prant.

Therefore, Ragho Ballal, the subedar of the province who after receiving the grievances from the peasant issued an order to his officer namely Ragho Bhaskar instructing him that be did not possess the power to collect such illegal and over tax from the Inamdar like Nilkanthrao. The Subedar prevented the officer from collecting such over-burdened taxes from the cultivators.

References and Footnotes

1. Khobrekar, V.G., Records of the Shivaji period, letter no. 17, p. 36.
2. Ibid., letter no. 17, p. 26. See footnote p. 40.
3. Ibid., letter no. 17, p. 32.
4. Ibid., p. 26
5. Ibid., letter no 17, p. 32.
6. Ibid., letter no. 17, pp. 31-32.

7. Ibid.
8. Ibid., letter no. 25, p. 62.
9. Ibid.
10. Ibid., p. 91.
11. Khobrekar, op. cit., letter no. 25, p. 62.
12. Ibid., letter no. 25.
13. Ibid., p. 63.
14. Ibid.
15. Shiv Charitra Sahitya (SCS) Part VIII, letter no. 26, Molesworth's Marathi-English Dictionary, p. 503.
16. Khobrekar, V.G , op. cit., letter no. 25, p. 62 (See footnote).
17. SCS, Part VII, letter no. 54, p. 81.
18. Ibid., Part VII, letter no. 50.
19. Ibid., Part VII, p. 115.
20. Ibid.
21. Ibid., Part VII, p. 78.
22. SCS, Part VIII, letter no. 84.
23. Ibid., p. 94.
24. Molesworth's Marathi-English Dictionary.
25. Ibid., p. 801.
26. Sambhaji Kalin Patrasar Sangarh (SKPSS) letter no. 237, SCS, VII, p. 81.
27. SKPSS, letter nos. 65-67.
28. Selections from Peshwa Daftar ed. by G.S. Sardesai, Part 31, 31.
29. SKPSS, letter no. 65.
30. SCS, IV, letter nos. 735, 736 to 739,
31. SKPSS, letter no. 2.
32. SCS, Part VII, p. 81.
33. SCS, Part III, letter nos. 523, 524.
34. SPSS, Part III, letter no. 2659.
35. Ibid., letter no. 2506.
36. SCS, Part III, letter no. 627.
37. SPSS, III, letter no. 2666.
38. SCS, Part III, letter no. 627.
39. SPSS, Part III, letter no. 2413.
40. Ibid., III, letter no. 2591.
41. Ibid., III, letter no. 2680.
42. Ibid., III, letter no. 2725.

43. SKPSS, letter no. 148.
44. SCS, Part VII, pp. 78 and 107.
45. SKPSS, letter no. 77.
46. Ibid., letter no. 16.
47. Rajwade, V.K., Marathyanchya Itihaschi Sadhane, Vol. XX, letter no. 241.
48. Bharat Itihas Sanshodhak Mandal's quarterly (Poona), First Year, p. 38, quoted in Kulkarni, A.R., op. cit. See chapter on village.
49. SCS, Vol. VII, pp. 107-108.
50. SPSS, III, letter no. 235. This document though belongs to the little early period of Ali Adilshah I, the King Shivaji would also have continued the grant of such lands to the Muslim inhabitants in the villages of his kingdom.
51. SCS, I, letter no. 20.
52. Ibid., I, letter no. 91; also see SCS, III, letter no. 403.
53. Ibid., III, letter no. 439, p. 55.
54. SPSS, III, letter no. 2686.
55. Ibid., III, letter no. 2506.
56. SPSS, III, letter nos. 2634, 2725, 2744, 2785.
57. SCS, III, p. 41 and also see SKPSS, letter no. 150.
58. Rajwade, V.K., MIS no. 150, Vol. VIII, 28.
59. SCS, I, letter no. 41 and also see SCS, IX, letter no. 69.
60. SCS, III, pp. 180 and 222.
61. SPSS, III, letter no. 2725.
62. Ibid., III, letter no. 2413.
63. Rajwade, V.K., M.I.S. letter no. 44.
64. Molesworth's Marathi-English Dictionary.
65. SCS, Part I, letter no. 81.
66. SCS, Part III, letter no. 427.
67. SKPSS, letter no. 150.
68. SCS, Part IX, letter no. 71.
69. SCS, Part IX, letter no. 71.
70. Ibid., IX, letter no. 76.
71. Ibid., IX, p. 75 (letter no. 69).
72. SPSS, III, letter no. 2466.
73. Ibid., III, letter no. 2594.
74. SKPSS, III, letter no. 232.
75. SPSS, III, letter no. 2379.

76. SCS, VII, letter no. 44.
76A. SCS, VII, letter no. 54, p. 86.
77. SKPSS, letter no. 87.
78. Ibid., letter no. 117.
79. Ibid., letter no. 241.
80. Ibid., letter no. 158.
81. SPSS, III, letter nos. 2478, 2499.
82. Rajwade, V.K., MIS, VIII, letter no. 28.
83. SCS, IX, letter no. 71, p. 78.
84. SCS, IX, p. 3 and p. 65.
85. SKPSS, letter no. 17
86. Sabhasad Bakhar, p. 26.
87. Maharashtra in the Age of Shivaji, pp. 106-125.
88. SCS, III, letter no. 401.
89. SCS, IX, letter no. 69.
90. Rajwade, V.K., MIS, XVI, letter no. 2.
91. Ibid., Vol. XX, letter no. 209.
92. Sanada Patre, p. 112.
93. Rajwade, V.K., MIS, XX, letter no. 10.
94. SPSS, III, letter no. 2468; also see SCS, IX, letter nos. 63, 91, 92.
95. SCS, III, letter no. 401.

3

Agrarian Condition of Maratha Kingdom

Agricultural Prices in Maratha Kingdom during 1630-1707 A.D.

The prices of all other necessary articles of life depend upon the prices of foodgrains. Their study helps up to properly understand the economic conditions of the people living in the society. In order to properly understand the socio-economic conditions of the people in Maratha country of the 17th century, the study of the rise and fall in food prices is necessary. In this paper an attempt is made to study the rise and fall in food prices in Maratha country during the pariod of 1630 to 1707 A.D.

The information about the prices of the foodstuffs in Maratha country found in our sources is certainly not abundant. But whatever data of food prices are available to us undoubtedly offer us an opportunity to analyse the economic condition of the Maratha country in some detail and make comparisons with conditions in the reign of Shivaji as well as in the later period of his successors. The present study also seeks to describe how the various factors interacted in determining the food prices prevalent in the Maratha country and thereby throws a new light on economic condition of the people under Shivaji that emerges from the available price data of his reign.

About the prices of foodgrains in the early period of Shivaji's reign practically we get very little information. The earliest reference so far known to the food prices prevalent in Maratha country in the early years of the 17th century is the food prices of the famine year of 1630. During this year the prices of grains rose to one hon per payali[1] (four seers).

These prices were two times higher than those obtained in prant of Supe during the famine year of 1657.[2] Of course, the price of grain in 1630 rose at an abnormal high level as it shows more than fifty-two fold increase in the normal price of grain as compared with the food prices of the year 1666 A.D. of Shivaji's reign. A comparison between the prices of foodgrains obtained in famine years of 1630 and 1657, shows that the food prices skyrocketted in Maharashtra in the former year and the famine of 1630 was one of the severest period of drought and most terrible famines known to the economic history of human society.

The prices of food articles of the year 1666,[3] 1676[4] A.D. prevalent in Maratha territories in the reign of Shivaji are found in contemporary sources and are given as under :

Article	*Weight*	*(Price in rukas)*	*Year*
Wheat	4 seers	11	1666 A.D.
Jwari	4 seers	11	1666 A.D.
Gram	4 seers	10-1/2	1666 A.D.
Rice	4 seers	5	1676 A.D.
Paddy	4 seers	2-2/5	1676 A.D.

The above quoted food prices are accepted as prlces prevalent in Maratha country of those years on the assumption that the food prices slightly differed from province to province in respect of variations in their local rates. It is obvious from the above price table of the year 1666 that the price rates of various articles of foodgrains like Jwari, wheat and gram did not differ much from the price rates from one another. Of course, the slight variations in the price rates in the markets of neighbouring provinces could be stated by difference in quality. The growth of food production could partly be explained by the extension of cultivation by bringing waste land under plough.

To promote the agriculture, the facilities like exempting peasants from land taxes,[5] for artificial irrigation etc., were provided by the king. With the aim of supplying water to the lands of peasants the dams, canals were also constructed by the State[6] The needy farmers were given loans,[7] seeds,[8] bullocks, and such other necessary agricultural equipment by the king. These administrative measures undertaken by Shivaji certainly brought the change in àgricultural conditions of Maharashtra and helped to increase the food production which brought down the prices of all commodities in the country. Despite the administrative measures and facilities provided by Shivaji, the cheapness of prices of foodstuffs cannot be denied due to good harvests.

Unluckily, prices of all major commodities of general consumption during the short rule of Sambhaji are not available. Only the prices of food articles like rice in Ashtagar province of the years 1681, 1685 86 and 1688-89, belonging to the early as well later days of Sambhaji's reign are available and are given below:

Grain	*Weight*	*Price*	*Year*
Rice	2-1/2 maunds	one rupee	1681[9]
Rice	9 seers	one lari	1685-86[10]
Rice	5 seers	one lari	1688-89[11]

For the comparison of the prices of the years 1681 and 1685-86, it is necessary to establish the relations between lari and a rupee in Maharashtra of the 17th century. The relations between lari and a rupee may be stated as below. It is found that one pagoda was equal to 10½ laris of the 17th century.[12]

A foreign traveller like Manucci[13] states that a pagoda was worth 3½ to 4 rupees. Therefore 3½ rupees or 4 rupees of the 17th century were equal to 10½ laris. Hence a rupee was equal to 3½ laris. Of course, this is a rough calculation. On the basis of the above calculation it can be said then that a lari of 1681 could purchase 25 seers of rice in the market. The documentary evidence records that the year 1685-86 of the same province was the year of food scarcity. But the markets in this prant were crowded with foodstuffs to such an extent that during this year the prices remained practically stable i.e. nine seers of rice was sold for a lari.[14] The important fact to be noted here in this connection is that the abundant supply of foodgrains from neighbouring provinces kept the food prices to level of normal prices. Again after two years this province of Ashtagar experienced a famine during which the price of grains rose very high. The rice sold in this province in 1688-89 was for two times than its price in 1685-86 and it was five times higher than its price in 1681 A.D.

Now a comparison between the price of rice in 1676 of Shivaji's period and that of Sambhaji is shown below.

Grain	*Weight* (in seers)	*Price*	*Year*
Rice	4 seers	5 rukas	1676
Rice	25 seers	per lari	1681
Rice	9 seers	per lari	1685-86
Rice	5 seers	per lari	1688-89

It is obvious from the above comparative price table that at the time of accession of Sambhaji the prices of food articles like rice were dearer than the prices prevalent during the year 1676 of Shivaji's reign. Hence the variations in the rates are certainly negligible. Thus on the basis of food prices of 1666 it can be presumed that the price rates of the commodities of food other than rice would not have differed much in their rates in 1676 also.

In examining the average level of prices of 1666 and 1676, there appears a considerable fall in food prices of the later year. The prices of the former year were comparatively higher than prices during the later ten years that succeeded the year of 1666. While searching the cause of price-inflation during the early days of his life, one has to take into account the political events that took place during the first twenty years of Shivaji's reign (1646 to 1666) of which the destruction of crops and food scarcity were the economic effects that lasted for two decades in the Maratha provinces. However, it is significant that on an average, the prices of foodgrains were appreciably lower in 1676 than in 1666. The cheapness of the prices of foodstuffs and the prosperity of the people in Maratha country can be guessed from the reasonable ground. During the first twenty years (1646-66) of his reign, Shivaji who founded the Maratha State had to wage wars not only against the Bijapuri enemies such as Chandrarao More, Afzalkhan, Siddhi Johar, but even against the Mughal Sardars like Shaistakhan, Mirza Raja Jaisinh. The expeditions or wars naturally affected food production in the country very badly and created food shortage and also the shortage of necessary goods thus raising their prices and helped to deteriorate the economic condition of the people during the period. But after 1670, it is probable that the Maratha country was enjoying the prosperity of abundant foodgrains. The increase in production of foodgrains was no doubt owing to the efforts and administrative measures undertaken for improving agriculture in the country by Shivaji himself.

A rupee of Shivaji's times of the year 1676 purchased three and half maunds of rice, whereas a rupee or 3½ laris of Sambhaji's times of the years 1681, 1685-86 and 1688-89 could buy two and half maunds of rice, 30 seers and 18 seers of rice respectively. From the comparative price levels, it is beyond doubt that the year of 1676 A.D. was the cheapest year as far as the price of rice in Maratha country is concerned. But soon after the year 1685 the prices again seem to have started rising. It meant that after a few years of the accession of Sambhaji his reign saw a considerable increase in the price of food articles like rice and other foodgrains also.

Even the price of cocoanut was dearer in the later years of Sambhaji's reign as compared with the price prevalent in the lifetime of Shivaji as well as in early days of his own regime. And this is substantiated by the following table of comparative price-levels of cocoanut during the period of Shivaji and in that of Sambhaji.

No. of cocoanuts	*Price (in taka)*	*During the year*
100	2-2½	1671[15]
100	2-0	1685[16]
100	5½	1686
100	6½	1687[17]

The price of cocoanuts was more or less in the period of Shivaji and that in the year 1685 that of Sambhaji. After 1685, the prices of cocoanut rose higher further during the last three years of his short rule and they were two or three times higher in 1687 than they were during the regime of Shivaji. It will be obvious from the above discussion that from 1685-86 onwards the prices in Maratha country started rising high up because of many reasons like the invasion of Mughal army on the Maratha territories like Belgaon, Dharwar, Miraj, Kolhapur, Panhala and on some provinces of north Konkan[18] the plunder by the Mughal and Siddhi's troops[19] and also natural calamities like famines etc.

Thus, on the average, the food prices of Sambhaji's period were comparatively higher. They were cheaper during the period of Shivaji as compared with the prices prevalent in the reign of his son Sambhaji.

Now the prices prevailed in the market of Kasba Akole of the year 1706 the last year of the period of Maratha War of Independence are available and are givn below.[20]

Article	*Weight (in seers)*	*Price (in rukas)*
Wheat	2¾	2½
Jwari	1½	1-1/4
Bajari	1½	1
Mug	2-2/10	2-1, 10
Urad (Mash)	1/4	2-3/4
Rice	7	6½
Chane (gram)	2½	2½
Ata Bajari	5 maunds	4 rupees

The price table of the market in Kasba Akole in 1706 shows that at the end of period of Maratha War of Independence the prices of foodgrains like rice came down more or less to the price-level of the year 1676 of Shivaji's period. The prices of other foodstuffs like Jwari, wheat and gram in 1706 also fell considerably and became cheaper as compared to those prevalent in the year 1666 of Shivaji's reign. Thus a comparison between the prices obtained in the early years of Shivaji (in 1666) and in that of 1706 shows a fall in the prices of foodgrains. But the invasions of the Mughal army on the Maratha territories, the plunder of the provinces by the troops of enemy, the expeditions undertaken by the Maratha against the Mughals etc. are the prominent features of the period of Maratha War of Independence. These wars and invasions would have destroyed the crops and created food scarcity which caused to increase the food prices at the abnormal high level and ultimately deteriorated the economic condition of the country. But from the food prices of 1706 of the Kasba Akole it appears that this year was a year of abundance and of good harvests. Hence it may be argued that this province remained away from the invasions of the Mughal army and the food production in this province did remain unaffected.

Now it would be interesting to compare the price of essential goods prevalent in the year 1719-20,[21] of the post-Shivaji period which are generally considered cheaper with those prevalent in 1676 of Shivaji's reign.

Kind of Corn	*Weight*	*Price*
Jwari	56 seers	1 rupee
Bajari	40 seers	1 rupee
Rice	18 seers	1 rupee

It can be said from the above mentioned price table that the rice in 1719-20 became seven times dearer than its price prevailing in the year 1676 of Shivaji's times and it was four and half times dearer than the price of rice in 1681 of Sambhaji's reign. Thus, it shows that the prices rose higher further during the period that succeeded the reign of Shivaji.

In taking a general view of food prices in Maratha kingdom, we can say that on the average, the food prices of the early lifetime of Shivaji were comparatively higher than prices prevailing during the last decade of his reign, i.e. 1670 to 1681. The price-inflation during the early years of his reign can be explained due to the fact that the early days of Shivaji's life witnessed several wars, the severest famines or droughts etc., due to which the prices rose very high. But probably, after 1670, when the Maratha State was stabilized, food production in the country grew considerably due to the administrative measures and agrarian reforms introduced by Shivaji. As a result, there was ample growth in supply of foodgrains which caused to bring down the price-levels in the markets of Maratha country. The phase in price-level of 1676 seems to have continued up to 1680 with minor fluctuation. But after five years of Sambhaji's ascendancy to the throne of Maratha state, the prices again started rising.

Thus, from the above discussion, it can be said that a number of factors such as the scarcity caused by natural calamities like famines or droughts the regional scarcity caused by difficulties and cost of transport of agricultural produce from one place to another etc., which affected food production in Maratha country, also interacted in determining the food prices in Maharashtra of the 17th century. Apart from these, wars and invasions of enemy's army play a vital role in determining the prices of foodgrains in Maratha country. It can be said that it was the law of demand and supply due to which the prices were determined in the period pertaining to Shivaji also.

Now the best thing for us is to compare the prices of food commodities of Shivaji's times with food prices of modern times.

A comparative statement of prices during Shivaji's period, vis-a-vis at present is given below.

Prices Then and Now

Commodities	*Prices in rukas per four seers (1666, 1676)*	*Prices in present century (1967) 7 kilos of modern times to roughly equal to 4 seers of that period (Prices in Rupees)*	*Ratio*
		Rs. Ps.	
Wheat	11	6-86	1 : 111
Jwari	11	5-67	1 : 99
Gram	10½	16-94	1 : 380
Rice	5	6-30	1 : 240

An average of the prices of these four commodities (i.e. 111+99+380+240=800÷4=200. We can say that prices of foodstuffs are two hundred times higher now than in the 17th century. We may say that on an average a rupee of Shivaji's times for general purpose, would equal in purchasing of two hundred rupees of present times.

Let us now consider the wages of workers of those days. In times of Shivaji the price-level of 1676 is a matter of great consequence to wage earners.

In Maharashtra of the 17th century, agricultural labourers, the artisans or the labourers were remunerated for their work by the allotment of share in grain produced in the farm that they served. The wages of unskilled labourer per day was one and half ruka.[23] But the rate of monthly wage paid to the lowest grades of workers like a coolie is recorded as 32 (thirty-two) rukas per day, by Carre, French traveller[24] who travelled in some provinces of the Deccan between 1672 and 1674 A.D. The servant like a clerk employed in fort of Shivaji was paid 3 hons per month i.e. 9 rupees per month.[25]

Compared to present standards, money wages of ordinary labourers or servants in Shivaji's time look extremely low. But this does not, however, mean that working classes in Shivaji times were poorer than they were in later times. And this can be shown by the following comparative table of wages paid during Shivaji period and in modern times of present century.

	Daily Wages		Monthly Wages		Ratio
	1672-76	*1967* *Rs. ps.*	*1672-76* *Rs. ps.*	*1967*[26] *Rs. ps.*	
Ordinary labourer			0-25	90-00	1 : 360
	1½ rukas	3-00	(one taka)		
Coolie	32 rukas	4-00	5-00	120-00	1 : 24
Clerk	57 rukas	8-30	9-00	251-00	1 : 28

An average of above wages 360+24+28=412÷3=138. This meant that wages of labourers and clerk are 138 times higher now than those of the wages in the 17th century. But prices of foodstuffs in Maharashtra are two hundred times higher in present century than in the 17th century.

The wages paid during the 17th century were smaller than those of present times. Their purchasing power was two hundred times greater than present day. The foodstuffs being so cheap in Shivaji's times, the real wages of labourers in fact were far higher than the wages earned by their descendants of the 20th century.

The conclusion is that poor classes and servants in Maharashtra of the 17th century had few wants which were met adequately from agricultural produce in the country. The clothings and living of the Maratha subjects were no doubt scanty and simple, but in respect of their food necessaries, the Maratha people had more to eat except during the period of scarcity or famines. Because the prices of the foodgrains were cheaper in proportion to their wages. From the above analysis of food prices and wages, it can be said that the period from 1670 to 1681 A.D. in Maratha history should be regarded as a period of prosperity during which the foodgrains could be obtained in much larger quantities by the poorer classes in society than the necessaries of life. Thus it would be fair to assure that the economic condition of the Maratha country under Shivaji was satisfactory. But it was certainly deteriorated during the reign of Chhatrapati Sambhaji.

Peasants' Problems in Maratha Kingdom

The Maratha rulers in the 17th century had fully realised the responsibility of the government to enhance the economic well being of the subjects. They showed great interest in working for the rural welfare and development. The efforts made by them to solve the socio-economic problems faced by the rural population in Konkan territory during the 17th century show that the Maratha kings took a lot of pains for the rural welfare.

The rural people in Konkan faced many problems of socio-economic nature. The foremost problem which they faced and which was to be tackled by the rulers, was the rural credit. There were no credit agencies providing financial needs of peasants in medieval Maharashtra. The cultivators obtained the credit from the usurer money lenders who were shete and Mahajan of the village.[27] The rate of interest charged on loan by the money lenders varied from 18% to 36%.[28] Sometimes, the rate of interest went high up up to 60 per cent also.[29] Hence many times, the debt of peasants increased beyond their paying capacity and became the double than the capital amount.[30] The absence of any other source of income except cultivation, the lack of production, uncertainty of rains, high land tax, destruction to crops by the enemy, all these factors brought limitations on peasants' ability to repay the debts. As a result, the debts of cultivators increased enormously. So the agrarian indebtedness in Mamle Cheul during the first decade of the 17th century became very acute and compelled some of them to sell their property of houses and lands.[31] We find that some of the cultivators in Cheul pargana were heavily indebted to the bankers.[32]

The over-burdened debts forced them to abandon their houses and villages also.[33] The peasants selling a part of their land to the Portuguese were prohibited by the government (of Muslim rule). The cultivators who sold the land to the foreigners without the permission of the government, were punished by sentencing them to the death also.[34] This rule might have been followed by the Maratha rulers as well. The sale of land to the Portuguese was forbidden by the rulers because they were anxious to see that the property of land should not pass from local peasants to foreign settlers. The kings thus discouraged the purchase of land by the outsiders for avoiding unemployment in agriculture.

Next problem that was happened to be faced by the rural men in Konkan, was the secured life or the problem of how to escape from impending danger of an external aggression. The Marathas had many enemies like the Siddhis, the Mughals and the Portuguese and the English etc. But the strongest was the Mughals. There was every possibility of the attacks on the villages by the enemies. So the problem of security of life of rural population no doubt required immediate attention of the rulers. Thus, in 1662, when the spies reported to the king Shivaji about the impending danger of an external attack on village people by Mughals, the king made the subjects aware of the danger of an attack and gave order to his officials to take them to safety places where defences were organized in order to meet the attack.[35] Likewise, the Siddhis when invaded Khed in Ratnagiri, the people were asked to take shelter into woods and mountains in order to escape from the ravages of the enemy.[36]

The peasants in Konkan had fluctuating fortunes in relation to the agricultural produce also. In the days of good harvest, Cheul,[37] Rajapur[38] and adjoining territory, produced the products like bettelnut, pepper, cocoanut, opium, ginger etc., abundantly and supplied them to European countries. During the 17th century, Javli, Kalyan, Bhivandi, South Konkan, Kudal, Sawant Wadi and such other places were the theatres of war and became restless places due to the struggles among the Marathas and their enemies,[39] and also owing to the movements of the army.[40] As a result, the crops in those regions were damaged and peasants suffered greatly. Consequently, the people had no other alternative than to bear the loss in agricultural produce and to face the problem of rising prices. Thus, when the English at Rajapur attacked and burnt Cheul in 1687, the production of cocoanuts and other plants were destroyed[41] and for the want of security the peasants left their villages. This seriously affected the agricultural production in the region and created the scarcity of essential articles whose prices depending upon demand and supply, fluctuated to a great extent. Thus, we find that before the invasion of the enemy on Cheul, the prices of cocoanuts and betelnuts were 5 takas and 9 takas per hundred respectively. But after the destruction of crops by the enemy, the prices of cocoanuts and betelnuts rose up to 6½ takas and 10½ takas per hundred respectively. This shows that the attack of the enemy caused the prices of the commodities to move high up and they were increased by 30% and 16% than their previous prices of the normal period.

Sometimes, undertaking the agricultural operations became quite difficult for peasants for the want of cattle. The scarcity of bullocks arose not only when the animals died during the famine period, but also on the occasions when the enemies burnt the villages and carried away the cattle of the peasants. Thus, for instance, when Mughal Sardar Shaibuddin Khan invaded the Konkan in 1682, he burnt twenty villages, killed four hundred men and carried away four thousand cattle.[42] Similarly the cattle in the villages on the frontiers of the Maratha kingdom were lifted by the enemy and this caused to cripple the whole economy of the villages.

Coupled with this, was another acute problem i.e. the rehabilitation of the deserted villages. The wars, the marching of the army, military activities of the soldiers, not only destroyed the agricultural produce, but also brought danger to the security of the life of common people. The peasants who felt insecured used to evacuate their home villages and went in search of livelihood elsewhere.[43] This resulted in depopulating a number of villages in the Konkan region also. The Siddhis and the Portuguese behaved excessively and caused much anxiety to the rayats in Konkan during the 17th century. We learn that the villages like Kude, Dapoli, Sidkoli etc , in Mamle Cheul were deserted in the year 1684 owing to the plunder by the Siddhis and the Portuguese.[44] Thus, the cultivators in village Pangotera in Kulaba district, when felt insecured, due to the attacks of the Siddhis, went to the neighbouring mountains for shelter with their families.[45] The Portuguese likewise the Siddhis, very often, attacked the villages,[46] burnt the houses,[47] destroyed the cultivated lands[48] and took away the subjects as slaves. Such activities of the Portuguese turned some of the villages into barren territory from where the people were migrated to distant places.[49] Hence the task of rehabilitation and reclamation of old villages in Kudal pargana as well as in other territories[50] was a necessary thing for the Maratha government which encouraged it by providing them land and giving them concessions in the taxes.

Sometimes, the forced labour (Vethbigari) which was an oppressive practice for peasants, created difficulties in cultivating their lands, and it forced some of them to migrate to other provinces and thus became an obstacle in cultivation of land. For instance, in 1685 the land in Mamale Cheul remained uncultivated because the rayats were engaged by government in other works which finally became responsible for lying their lands fallow.[51] So, to get rid of this oppressive practice, peasants in that pargana fled to other places like Revdanada, letting their lands to remain uncultivated[52] and thus they suffered economically to a great extent. In fact this situation adversely and deeply affected the cutivation and total agricultural produce in the country. In such circumstances, the state under Shivaji and his followers, adopted definite policy to mitigate the problems. On such occasions, efforts were made by them to increase the produce of land by encouraging the rehabilitation in the field of agriculture. They undertook certain compensatory measures like granting concessions in revenue tax to peasants and extending them government help in form of loan for purchasing the cattle and necessary agricultural equipment. The seeds for sowing at second time[53] was given to them. King Shivaji encouraged the cultivation by giving orders to his officers to advance loan to needy peasants without charging the interest and it was to be recovered in easy instalments from them.[54] The agricultural produce was increased by bringing new land under cultivation.[55] Likewise his father, Sambhaji,[56] had also extended necessary help from government in form of 50 Khandies of grain for sowing purpose to the rayats in Cheul pargana whose crops had been destroyed by the enemy in the year 1684. The Maratha rulers also afforded irrigation facilities for agricultural operations and encouraged the peasants for irrigating their lands.[57]

In fact, the Maratha Government in the 17th century provided every possible assistance to the rayats in villages in form of tagai loans, interest free, to the needy peasants or Government loans charging a lower rate than what was prevailing in those days, and also made reduction or gave concessions in revenue tax. The rulers made every possible effort to protect the people against the attack of an enemy and also induced the peasants who run away from their villages to resettle on their lands by giving them concessions in taxes,[58] or by distributing land among the new settlers of those villages.[59] The Government also gave exemption to the cultivators from the vethbegar when their agricultural operations such as cultivating the lands, watering or manuring to trees etc., suffered to a great extent on account of forced labour.[60] The Maratha rulers were paying much attention to rural development and were interested in securing well being of the people in their kingdom in the 17th century.

Famines and Famine Relief Measures

The discussion deals with the famine policy of the Maratha State under Shivaji and his successors. It is commonly believed that the Maratha rulers had no famine policy to guide the state. For example V.A. Smith says that:[61] "The ancient governments, Hindu or Muhammadan, did nothing as a rule in the way of famine relief. According to him the definite famine policy may be said to the date from 1877 A.D.

According to British Resident Charles Warre Malet, "The Maratha rule failed to promote the prosperity of society."[62] To him welfare subjects was no consideration with the Maratha (Peshwa) administration.[63]

But the facts mentioned below would prove contrary to the statement made by Smith and Malet. The Maratha State had a concrete sense of relieving the distress of the people suffered from famines. In fact it is obvious from the mass of evidences scattered in contemporary sources that Shivaji and his successors followed the famine relief principles defined in the ancient Hindu books and considered the subject as a part of the state policy and to be of sufficient importance. The picture that emerges from the evidences clearly reveals, that the practice of remitting taxes in hard times, providing employment to the people affected by famine, providing facilities of irrigation and granting government loans to peasants during the days of famine etc., which in modern times are considered as of government duty were also considered as a part of state policy during the period under review.

Famines in Maharashtra

Before going to study in detail the famine relief measures taken by the Maratha rulers it will be worthwhile to give some description of famines that occurred in medieval Maharashtra and created famine condition in Maratha country. The influence of famines on social and economic life of the society was great and this can be borne out by the facts described below.

It is evident from our contemporary sources that several famines occurred in Maharashtra during the 17th and the 18th centuries. The failure of rain or excessive rain or the wars were the causes of famine. The war disturbances, invasion of enemy's army, encampments of troops in the fields were other causes of destruction of crops. The destruction of crops was ultimately responsible for leading to famine condition.

A severe famine which occurred in prant of Supe during the period of Shivaji was a famine of 1657.[64] This famine caused the grain to become so dear that two payalis (eight seers) of grain could hardly be bought for a hon. Innumerable people died of starvation. This situation became so worst that it compelled a Desh-Kulkarni to sell a village for twenty hons only. Even the hungry mothers ate their own children for want of food. We read another worst type of famine which occurred in some parts of Maharashtra in 1686 and 1687.[65] The impact of famine was so severe that the villages were depopulated due to the deaths of innumerable people. Among the severe famines that occurred in Maharashtra during the Peshwa period a famine of 1753 is notable and is described in a ballad of Ram Joshi.[66] It caused the scarcity of foodstuffs and also affected the food prices severely. The price of one seer of jaggery was equal to the price of one tola of gold. One pie bought only one grain. The diamond had no value and no demand and its prices had highly declined. Another famine that occurred in southern Maratha country in 1787-88 was of unprecedented severity.[67] It caused misery to poor and rich both. Some people of upper classes who did not eat animal flesh and were unable to obtain grain at high price ended their lives by poisoning themselves, while the poor classes found scanty subsistence from roots, herbs and dead animals and even human corpses. Altogether twenty-five thousand persons were said to have died from starvation in the district of Gokak alone. The famines of 1790,[68] 1791, 1792 and 1793-94 produced disastrous effect on the crops in Ratnagiri, Ahmednagar, Poona and Junnar districts.[69] A war which was fought between the Peshwa and the Nizam in 1794 caused a severe famine in prant of Barsee.[70] The famine of 1803-04 made the situation so worst that numerous men died for want of food and some people cooked and ate their own children.[71]

Thus from the description given above, it is clear that the famine affected the socio-economic life of people greatly.

Famine Relief Measures

It is worthy to note that useful as well as helpful measures were adopted by the Maratha Government to meet natural calamities and the hard conditions of the subjects. Shivaji provided loans to peasants for purchasing necessary requirements like bullocks and seeds etc., during the period of distress.[72] Similar measures were adopted by his son, Sambhaji for relief of distressed peasantry in Cheul province (1687), when there was a famine on account of the plunder by the enemy. The intensity of famine was such that it resulted in the depopulation of Cheul town. Prince Sambhaji, therefore, ordered his officers to advance loans and provide bullocks, houses etc., to those people in Cheul who lost their possessions during the famine period.[73] He, realising the financial need of peasants, borrowed a loan of fifteen hundred pagodas from the French of Rajapur to meet the expenses incurred for providing the facilities to the sufferers.[74] Similarly, the Peshwa Balaji Bajirao advanced a large amount of loan to the several people of Balkwada and Jalalabad parganas in Bijagad district where famine occurred during the year 1747-48.[75] These facts are adequate to show that the Maratha state followed the policy of providing government monetary aid and necessary agricultural implements to the affected agriculturists.

Another necessary and helpful measure adopted by Shivaji was to provide the facilities in the form of remission of land revenue to peasants during the times of scarcity.[76] Likewise, Sambhaji granted remission of land tax[77] and the taxes on traders[78] when a famine causing much suffering to his subjects, visited some of the provinces in Maratha country in the year 1687 A.D. It was an accepted practice with the Peshwa Government to grant remission of land revenue to the villagers affected by famines.[79] Sometimes, the revenue amount due from the people was reduced for a period of some years.[80]

Next and the most important measure from the point of view of necessary and urgency was the distribution of food and clothes to the distressed. When a disastrous famine occurred in Poona and Junnar districts in 1792-93, the immediate relief was given by the State to the sufferers by distributing food to them.[81]

Ten years later some regions in the Maratha country had similar experience of severe famine on account of which the people of famine stricken areas migrated to other places like Kolhapur. It is recorded in the British historical writings[82] that during this period the contemporary ruler of Kolhapur (King Shivaji) made provision for distribution of boiled food to starving emigrants who had come to that capital town from other provinces.

But only the government loans provided to peasants could not solve the chief problem of the scarcity of foodgrains in seasons of drought and consequent failure of crops. The way in which the Maratha rulers dealt with this problem is clearly reflected in our historical records. To solve this difficulty they adopted another essential measure of importation of goodgrains from other places to the provinces where the food shortage existed. The Prince Sambhaji who seems to have fully recognised the necessity of maintaining the supply of grains in the affected regions and keeping their price stable in times of scarcity, imported foodgrains from neighbouring ports and trade centres like Surat and Ahmedabad.[83] A letter sent by the English of Bombay to the British officer at Surat furnishes that Sambhaji prohibited the import of foodgrains from his territories to English places. For this purpose he appointed his men to watch the activities carefully.[84]

It may be said that the primary motive of the Maratha ruler behind the prohibition of import of grain from his territories undoubtedly was to maintain the equilibrium of supply and demand of grains in his kingdom in times of distress and to avoid the danger of scarcity. Hence nobody will deny that prohibition of exports of foodgrains would have kept down the food prices in the Maratha country. The Peshwa government encouraged the traders to import grain by sea or by land from other places to the affected provinces on promise of remitting the octroi duty payable on the import.[85]

The Maratha State had many store-houses where the grain was stocked. The government stores provided seed grain for sowing purpose and cheap grain to poor peasants during the period of scarcity. This is clear from the fact that when Cheul province had been victim to the extreme food scarcity caused by the plunder by the Siddhis and the Portuguese—in the second and third years of Sambhaji's reign (1682-83), Nilo Moreshwar, the officer of the Maratha King distributed the fifty Khandies of grain which was collected from subjects and stored in government store-house at Sagargad to the affected peasants in the province for sowing purposes.[86] Thus the State granaries proved very helpful to the subjects in times of famine.

Another remarkable measure of the famine relief of the Maratha period was the making of provision for the employment to the distressed. During the Peshwa period attempts were made by the government to relieve the distress of the people by employing them on the work of public utility.[87]

Relief activities to be undertaken by the state in the field of charity were also not lacking. The charitable works done through the monasteries, which received the aids from the state also played a notable part in providing relief to the poor and the distressed. The government granted village inams to such monasteries. Shivaji, for instance, granted inamland for the maintenance of a feeding house attached to the Math of Monibaba of Patgaon.[88] We read that Chhatrapati Sambhaji gave village inam to Shri Devswami of Chinchwad who was doing charity by opening free kitchens of distributing food to the poor and satisfied the wants of the hungry.[89] He also made the gift of five hundred hons every year to the monastery of Mauni Gosavi at Patgaon for doing the charitable acts.[90] From other historical records we learn that Shivaji II who granted village inams to the Math of Turtgiri Gosawi through which the provision of distributing food to the poor was made also practised the charity.[91] From these evidences it cannot be denied that the charity activities of the state helped to lessen the suffering of the poor destitute persons to such extent that many of them would have saved from falling victims to hunger of starvation.

Likewise the government, private individuals also undertook the relief works. The role played by private initiative in saving the affected people from starvation was notable. We read that the Maratha Sardars like Nimbalkar opened aims houses for feeding the poor in times of famine.[92]

Again some generous merchants also lent their aid by distributing food and clothes to the poor during the hard times of famine.[93]

It appears that the Maratha state also did not neglect the irrigation works for fighting the famines. With a view to afford irrigation facilities for agricultural operations it took interest in permanent measures of excavating canals, constructing dams, digging tanks, wells etc. Shivaji, the founder of the Maratha state encouraged his people to construct dam on the streams in order to supply water through canals for irrigating the fields.[94] As far as possible he encouraged the canal works by granting the Patil inams of the villages to the private individuals who undertook the works. A dam constructed on river Banganga in Nasik region would have fairly served as a source of water supply for bringing the surrounding lands under irrigation.[95] It seems that during the times of Sambhaji the practice of erecting dam of rivulet and providing that water for irrigating the lands was also encouraged by the state.[96] The document which furnishes that the construction of a dam on Mohol's rivulet began in 1682 A.D., and it took eight to nine years to finish the work. The state under the Peshwas encouraged the irrigation by permitting the cultivators to construct a water-course from a rivulet for irrigating their fields.[97] The contemporary records show that the state constructed huge dams for irrigation purpose during the regime of Peshwa Madhavrao.[98] The Peshwa government not only itself constructed irrigation dams, canals, tanks etc., but also encouraged the private individuals by giving lands in inam in this connection. Thus, Ragho Narayan Kulkarni in Bagalan prant who intended to turn four hundred bighas of land into irrigated land by constructing a new dam on the river was granted forty bighas of land in inam by the government.[99] Sometimes, the state paid half amount of the total expenditure of the construction of a new dam and remaining half was collected from the cultivators whose lands were to be irrigated.[100]

The maintenance and repair of irrigation works was the responsibility of the state which took necessary steps for doing that. Usually, the government ordered its officers to repair the old dam by borrowing loan from the banker.[101] Thus, when the old dam in Bagalan province was damaged, the Kamavisdar of prant made a request to the government to grant some inams of lands to the banker from whom he wanted to obtain the amount of repairing cost by loan. We find that the government granted the above stated request of the officer.[102]

As regards the magnitude of the problem, the relief measures taken by the government to relieve the suffering of the subjects can hardly be considered as unfair and inadequate when slow communication, lack of modern means or fast land transport like railways, the existing conditions of those days and constant wars with the enemies etc. are taken into account. It must not be ignored that even the British rule could not provide sufficient relief to the mass of people during the famine period and a large number of people in villages suffered from famine conditions and scarcely could get a square meal.[103]

It will be seen from the details discussed above that several measures of great importance concerning the famine relief were implemented during the Maratha period as a part of state policy. The Maratha rulers made as many efforts as were possible under the conditions existing at that time to relieve the suffering of the subjects. What is more important for us to assert with greater confidence is that the Maratha rulers gave serious consideration to the natural calamity of famine and also to the necessary steps to be taken, to combat its effects. Thus, all that can be said in the light of historical facts is that the views expressed by British writers stated in the very beginning are groundless and incorrect.

The conclusion is, therefore, inescapable that in constructing canals, dams and tanks the Maratha State certainly contributed to the methods of fighting famines. The rulers took interest in irigation works which are the essentials of a sound famine policy. They had also adopted the measures of controlling the prices.[104] And with a view to relieve the distress, enough quantity of grain in state granaries was stored up Thus, the State carried all modern methods of fighting famines and practising various modes of relief. Therefore, it would be unjust to blame the state for not undertaking the proper relief activities or for not adopting substantial measures to prevent the natural calamities like famines.

Agricultural Techniques and Implements in Maharashtra under the Marathas

The present study aims to give an account of production technology of agriculture, with actual process of different techniques involved, and the mechanical elements used in agricultural production of Maratha country during the 17th and 18th centuries. The discussion intends to find out as to what was the state of agricultural technology in Maharashtra under the Maratha rule? What kind of technique did the peasants adopt for preserving and sowing the seeds, for planting trees, for increasing the fertility and yield of land and also for water conservation? How far agricultural technology in Maratha country suited to the needs of the people? In the 17th and 18th centuries agriculture was the main industry in Maratha country and other village industries were very closely connected with it. So raising of the status of the people mostly depended on the development of agriculture only. And to achieve this purpose, peasants made efforts by using their ancestor's agricultural techniques and implements, some of which they employed, were introduced in England only in last century.[105]

The agricultural technology of Maratha country was determined by those factors such as the situation of peasant farming, variation in climatic conditions in different parts, different types of land suitable for different crops in different areas, different amount of rainfall in different regions etc. which largely helped in determining the productive efficiency in agriculture.

The techniques of sowing into the soil was skilfully practised by peasants in medieval Maharashtra. While sowing the seeds the fertility and suitability of the soil for different crops, selection of proper seeds, amount of rainfall in the region etc., all these factors were taken into consideration. It is evident from the British Collector's reports that the agricultural operations were carried on after verifying the quantity of rainfall required for the cultivation of different crops. Soil was sown when considerable fall of rain had taken place and if there had been no ample rain, no grain had been put into the ground.[106] If little rain fell in light soil, the people sowed the crops like bajra[107] and there was little hope of producing other crops.

The technique of sowing proper crops in proper soil in proper season was used in practice. The Maratha rulers propagated for practising this technique by inducing peasants for sowing the rabi crops in the fertile soil and preventing them from sowing the kharif crops like karadi in the soil with great fertility in the rabi season.[108]

Harvesting twice a year was current in some parts of the country. The fertility of the soil was taken into account for growing two crops in a year. The cultivators in those parts where irrigation facilities were available only could cultivate two agricultural crops in a year. The rice, jwor, bajra, nagali, cotton, blackgram, mug, tur, groundnuts, seasamum (til) were cultivated in Desh region during the rainy season[109] (kharif crops). While wheat, gram, vegetable etc. were sown during the winter on the same field (rabi crops). Thus, the Maratha territories did not remain far behind in the multiplicity and variety of products of soil, and peasants fully utilized the knowledge of the suitability, of distinctive traits of the soil for growing different types of crops in different seasons. In watered and superior rice land, a second crop of peas, gram and wheat was raised.[110] Sugarcane was also grown on the same rice land and was followed either by jwori mixed with tur or nachani or sweet potatoes and vegetables,[111] in succession from season to season. This rotation system not only increased the soil supply of organs but also helped to control the diseases and pests.

The method of mixed cropping was common in Deccan where oil plants such as til, the Imvus, the Kareel, Kusde etc., were cultivated in fields either singly or mixed with grains.[112] Likewise, tur and umbaree were sown with grains like jwori and bajree,[113] but in such combination bajree or jwor was considered as main crop and tur and umbaree subsidiary. These combinations which fully utilised the properties of the soil, helped to increase the total produce by raising various crops. Among the irrigational crops, rice was grown at first in a nursery bed and then transplanted in the wetfield. Dr. Hove, a foreign traveller visited the Konkan coast while travelling from Surat to Bassein in 1787-88 and observed the process of rice-transplantation. He says, "in the beginning of the rains, the peasants sowed in a level in field a certain quantity of rice very thick, when it was grown to the height of five or six inches, they transplnated it into small tuffs into the other fields as soon as the rain permitted them.[114] This method saved a considerable quantity of seeds and also brought a triplicate crop to the farmers. Thus, the cultivators in Maratha country used the advanced technique for planting rice.

The peasants also cultivated cash crops like sugarcane, cotton and tobacco. It is interesting to note that the cultivators in Maratha country had accepted a new crop like tobacco and maize (macca) for the cultivation. The cultivation of tobacco had begun in Maharashtra since the sixteenth century. It was extensively grown in southern parts of Maharashtra especially in the territory belonging to Patavardhan in the 18th century.[115] The cultivation of maize seems to have been in existence in Maharashtra in the 17th century also.[116]

The technique of preserving seedgrains was well advanced. During the 17th and 18th centuries, in place of rock cut cells granary buildings nearly 30 feet in height,[117] were constructed. Those buildings proved helpful in protecting seedgrains from rats, insects,[118] ants and preserved the seeds in good condition.

Technique for manuring the soil was also practised by peasants who were well aware of its need for promoting the growth of crops. To manure the soil flocks of innumerable sheep and goats were kept on the plots for more than two nights continuously.[119] The urine and excreta, containing all the essential nutrients like nitrogen, potash and phosphoric etc., were observed into the soil and finally resulted in increasing the humus which undoubtedly contributed to the fertility of the soil. The peasants observed different kinds of practices for making manures. The good quality manure could be made by collecting straw, stubble, ashes, refuse of vegetables, other rubbish in a pit and mixing with cowdung and absorbing animal urine.[120] The excellent manure was formed when cowdung was mixed with the ashes of burnt branches and leaves of trees.[121] The valuable manure could be made by mixing and absorbing excreta and urine of large flocks of sheep with the ashes and was applied to garden land.[122] Irrigation by means of dams, tanks, lakes and wells were practised in Maratha territories.

The canals by short lengths running to carry water for agricultural purposes were in existence in those days. The canals excavated by the Maratha rulers have not been studied so far from technological point of view. Usually dams were earthen embankments some of which suffered from certain defects like leakage of water and were to be repaired after some years.[123] Dams that were laid across the openings of catchment areas, had sluices, the mechanical contrivances by which water was let out from the main canal into other branches or to feed the acqueduct.[124] Tanks were with few exceptions, natural rocky hallows and pits or narrow basins[125] varied from hundred to eight hundred yards in length, between hills which had been blocked together by a rude equipment.[126]

Reservoirs built at Jejuri by Tukoji Holkar[127], lakes built by the Bhosles such as Ambazari and Telinkhera near Nagpur, Parvati and Ketraj lakes etc., were built in stone and mortar masonry and are the best examples of excellent masonry work of irrigation system in Maharashtra in the 18th century. The sluices were constructed out of stone and masonry,[128] and provided water for crops, orchards and gardens.[129] In some parts of the country, wells used for irrigation were simple holes dug in the soil,[130] and were generally 8 to 10 feet in diameter and 20 to 25 feet deep,[131] unfaced with any building material. But in other areas, wells were pitched with brick or stone and mortar. Usually they were linked with dry cut stone and frequently were built only on the side on which the bag worked.[132]

Water Lifting Devices

In Maratha country, irrigation from wells by means of leather baskets[133] was the most common practice observed by the farmers. In provinces like Ratnagiri in Konkan region, the first type of device that was used in practice was 'the balanced bucket device' with a counter weight and was known under the name Lat. It consisted of long beam supported by upright forked post with a bucket attached to one end by means of a long bamboo and sufficient weight at the other end was secured to raise the bucket when filled with water.[134] Another kind of device that was used for water lifting was the leather bucket raised by wheel by means of cattle power. In this type, the water was raised in a leather bucket or mot which was two feet broad and was strenched open at the mouth by an iron ring. The other end was not stretched but was much narrower. A thick rope was fixed to the centre and was passed over a small wheel. A second thinner rope was fastened to a yoke drawn by oxen.[135] Water tower (storage-tank) with Persian wheel worked by bullocks was also used for supplying water to gardens and horticulture and it was another means of water lift. It was constructed in bricks masonry and was 50 feet in height. Its mechanism was based on the principle of syphone, i.e. that water always keeps its own level. But the Marathas were not the first to apply this principle as it was also applied earlier in Deccan Muslim kingdoms in 15th and 16th centuries.[136]

The king Shahu, his Peshwas and Brahmendra Swami made a substantial contribution to the growth of horticulture in Maratha country. They did so by applying the practice of grafting and the technique of plantation. The cultivation of rosy guava,[137] and varieties of mangoes[138] in different parts of the country was encouraged by importing and providing their plants to peasants. The seeds, the plants of oranges, cypress trees were imported from the Mughal territories[139] and were planted at Poona, Dhawadshi.[140] During the regime of Peshwa Bajirao I, the practice of grafting for good quality of mango was propagated. The plants of Balasad mango were brought from Gujrat and their cultivation was encouraged by means of grafting. Many different fruit trees were cultivated and developed by means of grafting in and around the provinces of Poona, Junnar, Satara, Balaghat and Gangathadi. It is, therefore, the 18th century was a period of considerable extension of cultivation of horticulture in Maratha country. The grafted plants were carefully brought from far off places by covering their root and junction of both plants with cerecloth[141] or a coating of mud.[142] The process of plantation was as follows—"The planter prepared the ground before the fall of rain and manured the soil with cowdung and set the roots at the depth of ten to fifteen inches. The plant when began to vegetate was heaped up furrows till the period of its maturity. Each plant received its necessary quantity of water regularly for its nourishment."[143]

Agricultural Equipment

Plough was made of babhul wood and was consisted of pole, share, yoke, tail and handle. In light soil, plough required two yoke,[144] but in stiff soil[145] heavy and large plough[146] was drawn by 7 to 10 yoke of oxen. Seedrill (pabhar) was consisted of two or four wooden iron shod shares called phans and seeds bowl in which seed was dropped by hand.[147] All the parts were held together by ropes.[148] Hoe (Kalav) was levelling instrument and consisted of two share or coulters joined by a level cross iron blade or phas.[149] Beam harrow or phal consisted of a large beam of wood fitted with a yoke, upright handle and was drawn by four oxen.[150]

Sugar Technology

Careri, an Italian physician who visited some parts of

Deccan in 1695 has recorded about abundance of sugarcanes planted at Bassein[151] and had observed a technique as well as the process of ripening and heating involved in the making of sugar. His account shows that the manufacture of sugar involved two types of technology. Firstly, the crushing of cane and secondly crystallization of juice. The first device was a sort of mill used for extracting juice from cane and was consisted of two wooden rollers turned about by oxen. This device involved the motion in opposite direction of two vertically mounted wooden rollers. The sugarcanes were crushed by being thrust between the rollers.[152] The cane juice when thoroughly squeezed out, was boiled in cauldrons and being cooled in earthen vessels at night, was crystallized.[153] The manufacture of sugar required technical skill for rapid boiling and speedy transference to evaporating pans etc. In some parts of the country, deep narrow copper pan instead of earthen vessel, was used for evaporating the juice.[154] Sugar technology seems to have reached at an advanced stage in the 18th century, because sugar constituted one of the important commodities of export of Maratha country to the port of Bombay.[155]

While summing up, it can be pointed out that the peasants in Maratha country employed simple and traditional implements and were unable to spend on advanced agricultural tools because of heavy burden of land taxes imposed upon them. They could meet that pressure by using skilfully their traditional technological knowledge and by handling carefully the rude equipment of agriculture. Though the agriculture technology of those times was less suited to commercial production it was not at all less useful. In fact, it contributed to make the villages self-sufficient in agricultural production, and also enabled them to supply surplus produce to urban population. Cities in Maratha country would not have grown unless there was a lot of agricultural surplus to feed a number of skilled workers and traders engaged in their crafts and trades in towns.

Agrarian Change in Maratha Country during the 18th Century

Change in any society can be related to political, socio-economical and cultural[156] The agrarian society in the 18th century Maharashtra was also not an exception to such type of changes. The discussion confines only to the study of a few economic changes which took place in agrarian field of Maratha country. It is true that there was no structural or fundamental change of western type in rural society of Maratha country but significant changes took place in different spheres of agriculture.

The signs of economic changes in the field of agriculture of medieval Maharashtra are visible in peasant cultivation of new crops and commercialization of peasant production, in extension of cultivation, in use of persian wheel for artificial means of irrigation, in extension of cultivation of horticulture, and finally in increased production of irrigated crops etc.

In addition to the crops like rice, wheat, jwori, bajree, naglee, gram etc., the peasantry in Maharashtra accepted and cultivated new crops like tobacco and maize (macca). The cultivation of tobacco had begun in Maharashtra since the seventeenth century. Tobacco cultivation which was of a comparatively recent origin and marginal utility in Maharashtra till the end of the 17th century, rapidly expanded during the second half of the 18th century. On account of the increase in consumption of that commodity by different classes in society like peasants, workers, artisans[157] and soldiers and feudal class of our period, the tobacco was extensively grown in southern parts of Maharashtra especially in the territory belonging to Patavardhan.[158] The instances found in contemporary records of the licences granted by Government for selling tobacco to merchants and traders in prants of Ravedanda[159] and Sashti[160] in Konkan region, a large number of shops established for selling tobacco in Poona[161] as well as in other towns and considerable income derived from it by the Government, suggest the increasing demand and marketization of the commodity in different parts of Maratha country.

Another economic change in agrarian field can be noticed in expansion of cultivation in different regions of the Maratha country. The agricultural expansion can be seen in the attempts made by Peshwa Government to increase production of food crops by converting dry land into wet field by means of irrigation facilities, or by reclaiming the fallow land[162] by granting half of land in inam[163] to peasants and by providing them tagai loan.[164] For instance, the extension of agriculture in Anjan-Wel taluka was made in the regime of Peshwa Sawai Madhavrao by bringing rocky ground under cultivation by covering it with the soil and by providing embankments around it.[165]

The extension of cultivation of cash crops like raw cotton and sugarcane etc., can be seen in commodity production of sugar and variety of cloths in different localities of Maratha country. Chandwad, Solapur, Nagpur, Akot, Balapur, Deulgaon Raja, Paithan, Khandesh and their adjoining territories, produced raw cotton on large scale.[166] The northern Deccan was characterised by increasing production of industrial crop like raw cotton. Textile was manufactured in provinces extending from Nagpur to Burhanpur.[167]

The crop of sugarcane was abundantly produced in the lands above the ghat or Desh tract in the 18th century.

The fertile soil in the regions of Bassein, Indapur,[168] pargana Junnar, Supe,[169] Satara, Sangamner pargana,[170] etc., was watered by wells as well as by canal water system connected with dam or tank and produced large quantity of sugarcane. The extension of cultivation of sugarcane in those regions during the 18th century, can be noticed in increase in quantity of export of sugar from Maratha country to the port of Bombay,[171] as is shown on page 80.

The effect of agricultural expansion can be measured in terms of increase in revenue rates. The revenue rates of rice

Year	*Maunds*	*Value in rupees*
1773-74	4526	3933
1777-78	7143	—
1779-80	1059	3177
1786-87	5633	19714

and wheat in prant of Mawal seem to have increased in the year 1745-46[172] than the rates of the year 1743-44,[173] due to the expansion of the area of cultivation.

Another major consequence of agrarian expansion and effects of irrigation works and of increase of food crop production like wheat, rice, raw cotton, sugarcane etc., was an increase in the activity of export trade of the country. The export trade of foodgrains of Maratha country was increased on a considerable scale in the 18th century. This can be shown by the evidence of Malet's report[174] which gives an account of commerce of the Maratha state during the years 1773-74, 1777-78, 1779-80 and 1786-87.

Article	*Khandies*	*Year*	*Value in Rupees*
Rice	7682	1773-74	92184
Rice	7855	1779-80	204230
Rice	17454	1786-87	191994
Wheat	09	1773-74	135
Wheat	439	1779-80	6585
Wheat	1781	1786-87	26715

The above given figures of increase of export of rice and wheat from Maratha country to the port of Bombay suggest the increase in food crop production and growing commercialization of peasant production in 18th century Maharashtra.

We find the following figures for the total value of goods exported from Maratha State to Bombay. They indicate the extent of trade of the Maratha country with the ports like Bombay.

The import of four years to Bombay from the Maratha state is as given below:

Period	*Total value (in rupees)*
1773-74 (from May 1773 to April 1774)	484835
1777-78 (from May 1777 to April 1778)	581680
1779-80 (from May 1779 to April 1780)	1104710
1786-87 (from May 1786 to April 1787)	877712

The increase in crop production may also be appreciably stated due to the improvements in techniques of agriculture like crop transplantation,[175] crop rotation,[176] manuring etc.[177] The Persian wheel[178] used for bringing water up from the wells can be regarded as important technological advance and contributed to the extension of irrigation in the country on considerable scale.

In sphere of irrigation, the significant development was the construction of dams,[179] canals tanks with sluices by which water was let out from main canals into other branches.[180] The sluices constructed out of stone and masonry[181] for carrying water for the crops, would appear to be a significant development of drainage technology. Dams were constructed for irrigational purposes through private as well as public enterprise.

The persons who constructed dams or dug the canals

and brought the land under irrigation, were granted the pieces of land in inam by the government. Thus, for instance, a new dam constructed by a person in 1770-71 brought 400 bighas of land under irrigation in Pisol pargana in prant of Baglan[182]

Lastly, the growth of horticulture in Maratha country in the 18th century can also be considered as noteworthy change in one of the various fields of agronomy. The practice of grafting and technique of plantation were applied in cultivation of rosy guava[183] and variety of mangoes[184] which was encouraged by the rulers by importing and providing plants to peasants. Likewise, the seeds and plants of oranges, cypress trees were imported from Mughal territories and were planted at Poona, Dhawadshi.[185]

The cultivation of good quality of mango was propagated and encouraged by importing the plants of Bansod Mango from Gujarat during the regime of Peshwa Bajirao I. Many different fruit trees were developed in and around the provinces of Poona, Junnar, Satara, Balaghat, etc., in the 18th century.

While concluding, it can be pointed out that to some extent the agrarian change in 18th century Maharashtra was the result of combination of State policy and economy, but many such changes occurred because of the adoption of new techniques in agriculture in the Maratha country.

References and Footnotes

1. Shiva Kalin Patrasar Sangraha, 1, 329.
2. Shiva Charitra Sahitya, Khand 7, lekh 44.
3. Shiva Charitra Pradeep, p. 109.
4. Shiva Charitra Sahitya, Khand 4, lekh 633, pp. 9-10.

5. Shiva Charitra Sahitya, Khand 8, letter No. 26.
6. Kulkarni, A.R., Maharashtra in the Age of Shivaji, p. 89.
7. Shiva Charitra Sahitya, Khand 9, letter No. 55.
8. Sabhasad Bakhar, p. 26.
9. Sambhaji Kalin Patrasar Sangraha, BISM, series No. 75, lekh 32, p. 10—the price of one khandi rice is stated as 8 rupees in this record.
10. Avalaskar, S.V., Angre Kalin Ashtagar (1947), p. 32.
11. Ibid.
12. Kulkarni, A.R., Maharashtra in the Age of Shivaji, p. 246.
13. A.R. Kulkarni, op. cit., p. 242.
14. Avalaskar, S.V., Angre Kalin Ashtagar, p. 32.
15. Marathyanchya Itihasachi Sadhane, VIII, lekh No. 26. It is found in this record that price of one khandi of cocoanuts was 125 laris. On an average the price of one maund was 6 laris. If we assume that a maund of the 17th century would be roughly equal to a quintal or 100 kilos of present century then the weight of two hundred and twenty-five to two hundred and fifty cocoanuts would be equal to one maund of that period. If the price of 250 cocoanuts was 6 laris then the price of one hundred cocoanuts was between 2-1/4 laris i.e. 2-1/4 takas of Shivaji's period.
16. Shiva Charitra Sahitya, khand 9, lekh 63, p. 64.
17. Ibid., lekh No. 69, p. 73.
18. Shivputra Sambhaji, by Kamal Gokhale (Marathi), pp. 309-312.
19. Ibid., p. 380.
20. Purandare Daftar, Part I, lekh 32.
21. Selections from the Satara Raja's and Peshwas' Diaries, II Peshwekalin Maharashtra, by Bhave, V.K., p. 199.
22. From Agricultural Prices in 1963-74.
23. Shiva Charitra Pradeep, p. 103.
24. A R. Kulkarni, op. cit., p. 214.
25. Marathyancha Itihasachi Sadhane, VIII, p. 29.
26. Maharashtra Civil Services (Revision of Pay) Rules 1969. Introduced under Government Resolution Finance Department No. PCR. 1269 dated 15th Jan. 1969, pp. 319, 356-57.
27. Shivkalin Patrasar Sangraha (SPSS) I, 482.

28. Khobrekar, Records of the Shivaji period, p. 209.
29. Shiv Charitra Sahitya (SCS) Part II, letter nos. 134, 352.
30. SPSS, III, 2466.
31. SCS, 9, letter No. 3; also see SPSS, I, 313.
32. SCS, 9, letter No. 21, p. 30.
33. SPSS, III, 2379.
34. SCS, 9, letter No. 3, p. 4.
35. Marathyanchya Itihasachi Sadhane (by V.K. Rajwade), XV, 276.
36. Kulkarni, A.R., Maharashtra in the Age of Shivaji, p. 281.
37. English Records on Shivaji, Poona, 1231, Vol. II, p. 325.
38. Ibid., Vol. I, pp. 277-79.
39. MIS, VIII, 26; also see SCS, II, 191.
40. SCS, 8, letter No. 26.
41. Ibid., 9, letter No. 69.
42. Kulkarni, G.T., The Mughal, Maratha Relations, Twenty-five Fateful years (1682-1707), p. 21.
43. SCS, II, 191.
44. Sambhaji Kalin Patrasar Sangraha, letter No. 117, BISM, Quarterly No. 75.
45. Abbe Carre, The Travels of the Abbe Carre in India and the Near East, 1672-74, ed. by E. Sir Charles, Vol. I, Hakluyat Society, London, 1947-48, p. 196.
46. SCS, 9, letter nos. 18, 19.
47. SCS, 9, letter No. 21.
48. Ibid., letter No. 18, 19.
49. SPSS, III, letter No. 2666.
50. Khobrekar, op. cit., letter No. 25.
51. SCS, 9, letter No. 63, p. 65.
52. Ibid., letter No. 20, p. 23.
53. Ibid., letter No. 55.
54. Ibid.
55. Ibid., letter No. 70.
56. Sambhaji Kalin Patrasar Sangraha, letter No. 123.

57. Kamal Gokhale, Shivputra Sambhaji, p. 392.
58. SCS, 8, 26.
59. Peshwa Daftar, ed. by G.S. Sardesai, Part 31, letter No. 10.
60. SCS, 9, letter No. 63.
61. Akbar the Great Moghal (1966), pp. 289-290.
62. Proceedings of Indian Historical Record Commission, Vol. IX, pp. 181-183.
63. Raghuvanshi, Indian Society in the 18th Century, p. 354.
64. Shiva Charitra Sahitya, Khand, 7, lekh No. 44.
65. Sambhajikalin Patra Sar Sangraha, B.I.S.M., Series No. 75, Lekh Nos. 205 and 234.
66. Y.N. Kelkar, Aitihasik Powade, I, p. 370.
67. A.T. Etheridge, Report on Past Famines in Bombay Presidency, p. 102.
68. Ratnagiri District Gazetteer, p. 370.
69. A.T. Etheridge, Report on Past Famines in the Bombay Presidency, p. 86.
70. Ibid,, p. 95.
71. Ibid., p. 86.
72. A.R. Kulkarni, Maharashtra in the Age of Shivaji (1967).
73. Shiva Charitra Sahitya Khand 6.
74. Dr. Kamal Gokhale, Shivputra Sambhaji (1971), p. 382.
75. Selections from Satara Rajas and Peshwa Diaries, III, Sanad 362.
76. Setu Madhavrao Pagadi, Chhatrapati Shivaji (1974), p. 47.
77. Shiv Charitra Sahitya, Khand 9, Lekh No. 71.
78. Sambhajikalin Patrasar Sangraha, Lekh Nos. 239 & 240.
79. Selections from Satara Rajas & Peshwa Diaries III, Sanad 360.
80. Ibid., Sanad 362.
81. Report on past famines in the Bombay Presidency, pp. 87 & 95.
82. A.T. Etheridge, Report on Past Famines in the Bombay Presidency, p. 101.
83. Dr. Kamal Gokhale, Shivputra Sambhaji, p. 487.
84. V.S. Bendre, Shri Chhatrapati Sambhaji Maharaj Yanche Vichikitsak Charitra (1971), pp. 336 and 340.

85. Selections from the Satara Rajas and Peshwa Diaries, VI, Sanad 743.

86. Dr. Kamal Gokhale, Shivputra Sambhaji, p. 425.

87. A.T. Etheridge, Report on Past Famines in the Bombay Presidency, p. 98.

88. Shiv Charitra Sanitya, Khand 4, pp. 88-89; quoted from Bharatiya Itihas Ani Sanskriti book No. 49, April 1976, p. 6.

89. Sambhajikalin Patrasar Sangraha, Lekh No. 88.

90. Ibid., lekh No. 202.

91. Tarabaikalin Kagadpatre, Khand 1, lekh nos. 101 and 161.

92. A.T. Etheridge, Report on Past Famines in the Bombay Presidency, p. 98.

93. Ibid.

94. A.R. Kulkarni, Maharashtra in the Age of Shivaji, p. 89.

95. Ibid.

96. Athalye Gharanyacha Itihas, Part I, lekh nos. 6 & 10, pp. 19, 29, 30; quoted from Kamal Gokhale's Shivputra Sambhaji, p. 392.

97. Selection from the Satara Rajas and Peshwa Diaries, VI, Sanad 742.

98. Ibid., VII, Sanad 427.

99. Ibid., VII, Sanad 426.

100. Ibid., VII, Sanad 427.

101. Ibid., VIII, Sanad 1016,

102. Ibid., VI, Sanad 641.

103. P. Sharan, The Provincial Government of the Mughals (1973), p. 407.

104. S.N. Sen, Administrative System of the Marathas (1976), p. 383.

105. Henry M. Eliot Memoris and C. of the Races of the North-Western Provinces of India Joh Beams (ed.) London, 1869, II, pp. 341-342, quoted from the Indian Economic and Social History Review, Vol. XVII, Jan.-March 1980, No. I, p. 3.

106. Report from H. Pottinger, the Collector of Ahmadnagar (1824) to William Chaplin, Commissioner, Poona, given in Selections from the Deccan Commissioner's Files (Peshwa Daftar): period of Transition (1818-1826) ed. by R.D. Choksey, pp. 18-20.

107. H. Pottinger's Report to William Chaplin, op. cit., p. 19.

108. Bharat Itihas Sanshodhak Mandal Qurly, XV, No. 2, Sept. 1934, p. 62.

109. Shiv Charitra Sahitya, 7, letter No. 67, SCS, 8, letter No. 26, SCS, 9, letter No. 69, Marathyanchaya Itihasachi Sadhane, XIV, Letter Nos. 62 and 91, and XXI, Letter No. 47, Peshwa Diaries, III Sanad 356.

110. Gazetteer of Bombay Presidency, Vol. XXIV, p. 168.

111. Selections from the Records of Bombay Government, No. II, Captain Wingate's report on Survey and Assessment of Ratnagheery, a letter from the Revenue Commissioner, H.E. Goldmid, p. 7.

112. Report on the Territories conquered from the Peshwa by Hon'ble Mount Stuart Elphistone Commissioner (1821), Appendix, p. III.

113. A Letter from William Chaplin Deccan Commissioner to the Collector given in period of Transition (1818-1826), p. 35.

114. Selections from Records of Bombay Govt. New Series, No. XVI, Tours for Scientific Research made in Gujrat, Kattiawar & Conkuns in 1787-88 by Dr. Hove, p. 13.

115. Bharat Itihas Ani Sanskriti Mumbai Marathi Granth Sangrahalaya Series Jan.-March 1979, Vol. 60, pp. 42-43.

116. Indian Historical Review, July 1978-Jan. 1979, Vol. V, No. 1-2.

117. Mate, M.S., Maratha Architecture, p. 52.

118. Saryu Doshi, Shivaji & Facets of Maratha Culture (1982), p. 52.

119. Bhave, Peshwekalin Maharashtra, pp. 159 and 373.

120. Statistical Report on the Principality of Kolhapur, by D.C. Graham, p. 53.

121. Captain Wingate's Report of Survey & Assessment for Ratnagheery, p. 7.

122. Statistical Report on the Principality of Kolhapur, by D.C. Graham, p. 53.

123. Peshwa Diaries, VIII, Sanad 1058.

124. Mate, M.S., Maratha Architecture, p. 43.

125. Studies in Indian History (ed. by V.D. Rao), pp. 170-171.

126. Statistical Report on the Principality of Kolhapur, by Graham, D.C., p. 83.

127. Mate, M.S.,'Maratha Architecture, p. 42.
128. V.K. Bhave, op. cit., p. 41.
129. M.S. Mate, op. cit., p. 42.
130. Statistical Report on the Principality of Kolhapur, by Graham, D.C., p. 83.
131. Gazetteer of Bombay Presidency, Vol. XVIII, Part II (Poona), p. 12.
132. Ibid.
133. Chapekar, N.G., Peshwaichya Sawalit, p. 47; also see Peshwa Diaries, III, Sanad 437.
134. Selections from Records of Bombay Government, Memories on Sawant Waree State by Major J.W. Auld, p. 44.
135. Gazetteer of Bombay Presidency, Vol. XVIII, Part II, p. 12.
136. Mate, M.S., Maratha Architecture, p. 45.
137. Selections from the Peshwa Daftar, ed. by G.S. Sardesai, Part 18, letter No. 177.
138. Bhave, V.K., Peshwekalin Maharashtra, p. 143.
139. Selections from Peshwa Daftar, Part 18, letter No. 177.
140. Ibid., Part 22, letter No. 214.
141. Selection from Peshwa Daftar, Part 18, letter No. 177.
142. Bharat Itihas Sanshodhak Mandal Quarterly, September 1934, Vol. XV, No. 2, p. 67.
143. Tours for Scientific and Economic Research made in Gujarat, Kattiawar and Conkuns in 1787-88, p. 11.
144. Gazetteer of Bombay Presidency, Vol. XVIII (Poona), p. 8.
145. Alexander Mackey, Western India, reports addressed to the Chamber of Committee of Manchester, Liverpool, Blackburn and Glasgow (London); quoted from proceedings of 43rd session of Indian History Congress 1942, p. 466.
146. Gazetteer of Bombay Presidency, XVIII, Part II (Poona), p. 8.
147. Science and Technology in Medieval India, by O.P. Jaggi, p. 219.
148. Gazetteer of Bombay Presidency, Vol. XVIII, Part II, p. 8.
149. Gazetteer of Bombay Presidency, Vol. No. XVIII, Part II, p. 9.
150. Ibid.
151. Guha, J.P., India in the Seventeenth Century, Vol. II, The Voyages of Thevenot and Careri, p. 203.

152. Proceedings of 43rd session of Indian History Congress (1982), p. 469.
153. Guha, J.P., India in the Seventeenth Century, Vol. II, p. 203.
154. Report on the Improvement of Indian Agriculture, London (1893), p. 226; quoted from Proceedings of 43rd Session of Indian History Congress (1982), p. 470.
155. From Home Department, 1789, Public Original Consultation, 22 April, No. 25 (Unpublished record).
156. J.S. Grewal, "Social Change in Medieval India", General Presidential Address, Indian History Congress, 45th Session, Annamalai Nagar, 1984, p. 3.
157. V.K. Bhave, Peshwekalin Maharashtra, p. 27.
158. Bharat Itihas Ani Sanskriti, Mumbai Marathi Granth Sangrahalaya series, Jan.-March, 1979, Vol. 60, pp. 42-43.
159. Peshwa Diaries, III, Sanad 464.
160. Ibid., Sanad 465.
161. Bharat Itihas Ani Sanskriti, Mumbai, Jan.-March 1979, Vol. 60, p. 43.
162. Ibid., Sanad 425.
163. Ibid., VI, Sanad, 737.
164. Ibid., Sanad 384.
165. Ibid., VI, Sanad 737.
166. Ibid., III, Sanad 458, VII, Sanad 716; also see V.K. Bhave, op. cit., p. 267.
167. Proceedings of Indian History Congress, Bodh Gaya (1981), p. 357.
168. Peshwa Diaries, I, Sanads 287, 289.
169. Ibid., VI, p. p. 254.
170. Ibid., Sanad 711.
171. From Home Department, 1789, Public Original Consultation, 22 April (No. 25) (Unpublished record) kept in National Archives of India, New Delhi.
172. Peshwa Diaries, III, Sanad, 358.
173. Ibid., Sanad 356.
174. From Home Department, 1789, Public Original Consultation No. 25.
175. Dr. Hove, "Tours for Scientific Research made in Gujrat, Kattiawar, and Conkuns in 1787-88, p. 13.
176. Captain Wingate's Report on Survey and Assessments of Ratnagheery, a letter from Revenue Commissioner, H.E. Goldmid, p. 7.

177. Statistical Report on Principality of Kolhapur, D.C. Graham, p. 53.
178. M.S. Mate, Maratha Architecture, p. 41.
179. Peshwa Diaries, VIII, Sanad 1058.
180. M.S. Mate, op. cit., p. 43.
181. V.K. Bhave, op. cit., p. 41.
182. Peshwa Diaries, VII, Sanad 426.
183. Selections from Peshwa Daftar (ed. by G.S. Sardesai,) Part 18. letter No. 177.
184. V.K. Bhave, op. cit., p. 43.
185. Selections from Peshwa Daftar, Part 22, letter No. 214.

4

Urbanization in Maharashtra during the 17th and the 18th Centuries

Forts, Monasteries and Pilgrimages : Factors of Urbanization

On the urban history of Maharashtra of the medieval period, a great deal of fundamental research work needs to be done. I have made some attempt at understanding the economic, geographical and political factors contributing to the urban growth in medieval Maharashtra in my research works.[1] The present discussion confines only to the study of the role of forts, pilgrimages and more importantly the presence of institutional forces like religious monastery, helping the growth of the small towns in Maratha kingdom during the 17th century. While studying the urbanization of early Maratha period, one finds that in some areas of the kingdom, the industrial and commercial activities were the major factors which helped the growth of the towns, while in other regions, the presence of forts, monasteries and pilgrimages was a necessary factor of the process of urban growth.

For understanding the prices of growth of urbanization in Maratha kingdom, one has to look at the evidences afresh to study economic function of the forts, quite distinct from their political and military role, helping the growth of urbanization. The another major concern in discussing the role of forts in urbanization is the study of urban characteristics of the capital forts of the Marathas. The urban features of two royal centres namely Rajgad and Raigad will be taken up for discussion and can be found in the explanation of their two aspects i.e. (1) Forts as royal centres and as the posts for protection of urban centres and trade (2) forts serving as the places of distribution of foodgrains into the markets. The early medieval urbanization in Maratha country, likewise in plain area, also seems to have located in hilly region of Konkan territory. Rajgad and Raigad the two royal capitals of King Shivaji certainly possessed the characteristics of a urban centre and town life. In case of Raigad much land on the fort was reserved for the reservoirs like Gangasagar[1a] for storing water, also for the headquarters of officials, number of buildings consisting of Government offices, royal palaces, eighteen Karkhanas,[2] Granaries, garden,[3] tank[4],shopping complex etc. All those were an integral part of town life and are certainly the visible feature of urban places of medieval period.

The urban features can also be visible from the remains of a number of buildings found at the fort of Rajgad, the first capital of King Shivaji, where residential quarters, State Offices granary, temples,[5] shopping[6] area and the system of water supply,[7] seem to have existed. The direct link between market places and forts was in existence. The grain stored on forts for sale or distribution[8] was released into the market places with a view to check the rising prices during the period of scarcity.[9] Moreover, the forts like Raigad and Purandar were the places of manufacturing activities of coins[10] and cannons,[11] which certainly added to their urban features. The mint of Raigad issued a considerable number of gold and copper coins. The linkages between gold coins and long distance trade going together and importance of copper coins for local trade cannot be exaggerated. There is one more sphere in which the forts assumed a dominant role i.e. in relation to the protection of urban centres and trade. The forts located on highways or trade routes or nearer to the towns provided defence to the urban places and trade. Some of the forts serving as guarding posts were so effective that they could stop the enemy on the highways, before he could reach and attack the town. On emergency occasions, the forts by sending detachment to the rescue of the town offered shelter to the urban subjects.[12] Thus, the forts of Sinhgad, Shivneri, Purandar, Raigad, Panhala guarded the routes leading to the urban centres and offered protection to towns such as Poona,[13] Junnar,[14] Mahad and Kolhapur[15] respectively. Forts on sea coast not only guarded the coast over long distance but also kept the sea route of trade safe.[16] Some of the strong forts built to command the water routes offered protection to port towns and also trade. The forts like Khanderi Undari, Kulaba, Yashwantgad protected not only the ports like Bombay, Alibag and Jayatapur harbour[17] respectively but also the trade conducted on sea-water.

There were some market places known as peths situated very close to the capital fort of Raigad. Thus, the peth of Pachad where the traders like Baniyas and Gujar settled, provided articles of daily life to the market established on the forts of Raigad.[18] It is likely that the trading places like Mahad a town very adjacent to the Raigad acted as a central urban complex of the small market places like Pachad and also the villages of Majare, Wadi, and such other places.[19] The fortifications of some of the towns like Poona, Kalyan and others helped the urban growth in Maratha kingdom in the 17th century. It appears that the urban complexes on hill forts in Maratha kingdom soon broke up after the Mughal conquest of the Maratha capital fort of Raigad and also with the shift of the place of capital from the fort to the towns like Poona, Satara in the plain area.

The second type of urban centre in those days was the town where monastery or the institution of religious cult was established.

To this category, may be assigned Chaphal[20] Patagaon,[21] Shingnapur, Kasbe Nimb,[22] Chakan,[23] Chinchwad[24] where monasteries of saint Ramdas and Mouni Bawa, Kamalnayangiri, Anandgiri and of Moraba Gosawi etc. were established. Some of the places where the monasteries were the major factor in their urban character also acted as market centres or kasbas. This meant in many cases the Marathas were either located in the kasbas or subsequently kasbas were developed around the Mathas. Thus, the Kasba places like Chaphal, Nimb, Shingnapur, Chakan etc. had the added prestige of being the places of market centres as well as the places of ceremonial centres of religious festivals which contributed to their urban growth. Such towns rose to prominence as urban centres in the particular region during the 17th century; because of their dual activities of religious and economic in nature. The major economic activities centering round the Mathas are reflected through endowments in form of land[25] and allowance of money for various purposes like religious festivals, ceremonies of fairs,[26] feeding of ascetics[27] and pilgrims, burning of lamps, performing the worship[28] etc. The Mathas possessed the movable and immovable property which was granted by the ruling class[29] or noble men. The Kasba Chaphal had a well known Math of Saint Ramdas and also a temple God Rama. It was a centre where religious festival of Rama Nawami, the birthday of God Rama was celebrated annually.[30] On such occasions, King Shivaji and his son Sambhaji were made special endowments to the Math.

The religious activity and the ritual needs of the shrines helped the town of Chaphal in evolving it into urban complex, a centre for selling the images of gods brought from Karnataka[31] for the temples. The Math at Chaphal undoubtedly helped to the growth of the town in size as the new settlements of Brahmin community came into being there during the 17th century,[32] The Mathas had rest houses and free kitchens. The places of monasteries became prominent because they were also the halting centres on pilgrim routes. Many pilgrims going to pilgrim centres halted at the Mathas where free meals were served to them. The Math of Mouni Bawa at Patgaon was the centre of the Nath cult where one thousand people were fed freely[33] every day. Patgaon situated on the bank of Vadgana, stood on the main route joining the port of Rajapur, to Kolhapur, Athani and then to Bijapur. It also connected the port of Kharepatan by the route passing through the pass of Phonda and going to Nipani and Rayabag.[34] It was one of the visiting places for many people who came to receive the blessings of Mouni Bawa, a spiritual teacher of King Shivaji. It is needless to say that the towns of Mathas certainly became the centres of a brisk of trade and commerce on the occasions of annual fairs or the celebration of religious ceremonies. Thus, the Mathas by assuming great significance from the time of the Bhakti movement in Maharashtra, certainly served as the basis for the growth of urban centres even in the 17th century. Other type of urban places in Maratha country were the tirthkshetras or sacred centres which grew due to their location on the banks of rivers and holy shrines of local importance. Such religious places which had acquired sanctity for centuries together and developed into centres of pilgrimage, served as trading centres during the 17th century also.

In such category the towns like Pandharpur[35], situated on the banks of Bhima river, Alandi and Dehu situated on banks of Indrayani river, may be noted. The place of Trimbak was one of the seats of twelve Jyotirlingas in India and was also sanctified by the temple of Nivrittinath, the guru and elder brother of saint Dhyaneshwar.[36] Pandharpur and Tuljapur were the towns with the holy shrines which attracted a large number of pilgrims from all over the country. Pandharpur, a town with the temple of god Vithhal and as a meeting place of all pilgrims, a centre of Bhakti cult, rose to prominence as a trading centre in the 17th century by becoming the pilgrimage of the Hindus. Similarly, a place with the temple of a goddess Bhawani attracted many devotees from all over the country. Kasbe Saswad which located near to the fort of Purander, assumed importance as a sacred place where the Samadhi of Shree Sopandev, the younger brother of Dhyaneshwar was built[37] and which held in high respect by the Hindus. The people who came to the towns of holy temples and samadhis, visited those places for the offering the worship. The temples of holy devotees or the samadhis in the towns, thus, encouraged the tourist activities in Maratha kingdom. The pilgrim traffic at the pilgrim places particularly on the occasions of religious festivals or fairs increased the trading activities of those towns and finally helped them to become popular and famous urban centres in Maratha country during the 17th century.

The above discussion thus giving the variations, as one can expect, in the pattern of urban centres in 17th century Maratha kingdom, shows that the forts, monasteries and pilgrimages were also the useful factors in bringing of the growth of small towns.

Urbanization in Maratha Kingdom during the 17th Century

The present discussion is an attempt to study the urbanization in Maharashtra during the 17th century. Not much attention has been paid so far to the study of socio-economic phenomenon of urbanization. It seems that urbanization, like in other provinces had taken root in Maharashtra too. Recent study[38] of economic life of Maharashtra under Shivaji throws a light on some trading and industrial centres of Shivaji's times. However, the study of the variables such as geography, polity and economy helping the process and growth of urbanization and also urban features that emerged in towns of Maratha kingdom in the 17th century remains a topic to be discussed. The focus of our study is, therefore, on the analysis confining to the general review of various factors those, either separately or together shaped the course of history of urban process and growth in Maharashtra during the 17th century.

In the contemporary Marathi records as well as in the factory records of East India Company, there are references to Rajapur, Dabhol, as flourishing trade centres under the dominance of Shivaji.[39] In his travel account Careri says, "all the coast from Cheul to Goa for the space of 250 miles belonged to Shivaji, he had several forts besides cities and towns."[40] Urban centres in Maharashtra of Shivaji's times appear to have flourished more in Konkan territories. Some of them like Cheul, Dhabhol, Chiplun, Vengurla were located at the points of communication like sea or river and others such as Poona, Junnar, Kolhapur on or close to the trade routes.

A few of these urban centres namely, Kalyan, Bhivandi, Cheul, Rajapur, Dabhol, Vengurla, Pen could be regarded as trade centres in importance only to Surat and Goa,[41] were port towns with inland and foreign trade. Throughout the 17th century Kalyan, Bhivandi, Panvel had flourishing industries of ship and boat building and also the crafts of weaving. They were the centres of manufacturing cloth like bleached cottons, sele and turbans.[42] The cloth manufactured at these centres was exported to Bombay.[43] Shivaji had his own centres of ship and boat building industries at Kalyan, Bhivandi and Panvel. The contemporary Portuguese records also speak of Shivaji's warships built at these centres.[44] He had employed the Portuguese ship-builders (Firangi) in the work of constructing warships. The ship building industry of Shivaji at Kalyan gave employment to about four hundred Portuguese artisans.[45] Upper Cheul seems to have another centre of ship and boat building industry in the 17th century where Shivaji built fifty warships at the centre in 1664.[46] The availability of abundant timber in this area helped these towns to flourish as ship building centres in the 17th century. There is no doubt that the ship building industry contributed to the growth of commerce and trade of Maharashtra in the 17th century.

Cheul was a place of trade and a manufacturing centre as well. Shivaji possessed this town in about 1670. It was famed for its silk fabrics and coloured clothes.[47] The weavers in the town made five thousand pieces of tafatties in a year.[48] It seems that the raw-silk required for silk weaving industry at the centre was imported from Bombay and Fattenagar.[49] We get reference to Cheul as urban centre in the accounts of foreign travellers. According to Dr. Fryer, the town was a great mart of all sorts of Deccan commodities in former times, but was ruined in the wars between the Mughals and Shivaji.[50] Thevenot says, the port of Cheul was difficult to enter but very safe and secure from all foul whether, it was good town and defended by a strong citadel upon the top of a hill.[51] Thomas Nicolls who visited Cheul in 1673 describes that the city had been furnished with fair buildings, but two-third parts of it were ruined, as a result, the town had also declined in its population considerably.[52] Cosmeda Guarda gives a fairly good idea of this urban town in the 17th century. To him, Upper Cheul was a great place inhabited by Mouras and Gentions, all rich merchants and there were many weavers with most curious merchandise. All worked hard and its great commerce made the land very prosperous.[53] The town served as a commercial centre not only of Maharashtra but also of India. It was a collecting centre of cotton textile goods from different parts of the country.

The variety of cloth coming from Balaghat, Kalyan, Bhivandi and coloured clothes coming from outside India and going to Balaghat, Kalyan, Bhivandi were collected at Cheul.[54] Saltpetre, pepper were procured here at reasonable rates,[55] It had flourishing trade with other ports like Rajapur, Surat and Bombay. It was a town where a rich and a large number of Gujarathi merchants and wealthy traders were living. Hence, in 1666, Shivaji had written to the Captain of Cheul to collect two lacks of rupees from the Gujarathi merchants of that town and send that amount to him as loan.[56] The above description of the economic activities of the town shows that Cheul exhibited urban traits at least in two respects. It was a town with fairly rich business community and was a centre of manufactures and commerce. The town had a mint where Cheul laris were struck.[57] It is but natural that the coins issued from the mint helped in developing the trade of the town. Thus, throughout the 17th century, Kalyan, Bhivandi and Cheul were the towns with industries and crafts and also the centres of production of manufactured articles. Hence no doubt grew in size and population. Thus, the industries and crafts played an important role in process of urbanization in Maharashtra during the 17th century.

Dabhol was a port town which Shivaji captured from the Mughals and made it a part of his kingdom in 1652. According to Careri, this city was in possession of Shivaji.[58] The port had a strong and handsome fort belonging to Shivaji.[59] It was an important centre of trade of pepper and salt during the 17th century.[60] In fact, it had become an important traffic centre for foreign trade as numerous ships loaded with goods sailed from this port to Iran, Muscat, and such other foreign countries[61] A mint was also located in the town and the coins issued from the mint were known as Dabhol laris.[62]

During the 17th century, Rajapur was another flourishing commercial centre of Konkan region. The French East India Company had established its factory at this place.[63] Rajapur came under the possession of Shivaji in 1664. As it is mentioned in the records of the English East India Company, Rajapur was as important commercial centre as Karwar in those days and here the goods were sold at cheaper rate by 20% than those of Surat.[64] Shivaji had sacked the English factory at Rajapur in 1660 and also in 1670.[65] It served as a centre for foreign import goods as well as for indigenous export commodities. Its vessels loaded with goods were sent to Bombay, Surat, Mecca, Iran, and Muscat.[66] The traffic in goods between Bombay and Rajapur was regular and consisted of commodities like pepper, cocoanuts, betelnuts, and clothes.[67] In 1660, Henry Revington had thought that Rajapur in future would be centre of large trade in saltpetre, pepper, callcoes, cotton yarn etc.[68]

Some rich merchants living in the town possessed their own ships which sailed to Red Sea, Basra in Persia.[69] Thus, the trading activities of Rajapur, its important position as commercial centre for inland and foreign trade and the rich merchant class living in the town etc., these features of the port indicate the urban growth of the town.

Vengurla was other important port town and a centre of trade both during the 17th century. It had the Dutch factory for cloth both fine and coarse.[70] In 1660, it was a large town with one of the best roads in India. Vengurla served as a commercial centre of coastal trade not only of Maharashtra but also for other parts of India. It was visited by many ships from Barsorlar as well as from the ports of Karnataka for taking in cargoes of rice and saltpetre.[71] The ships laden with salt from this place were taken to Maneri.[72] The ships from Batavia, Japan, Bengal, Ceylon visited this port and its vessels loaded with goods were sent to Surat, Ormuz, Basra and the Red Sea.[73] The trade of Shivaji with the Arab countries was conducted through this port. The Marathas brought the merchandise from Karnataka at this centre and loaded it on their ships bound for Muscat.[74] A mint which issued Nishani hons was also located in the town[75] The political factor unlike the geographical, economic factor also contributed to the growth of this town. Dicholi was a big town of the Maratha ruler, Sambhaji. It was a place where the English, the French, the Dutch and the Portuguese merchant communities had established their houses.[76] When the Mughals made an invasion on Dicholi in 1684, the town was plundered and burnt by the army of Aurangzeb. This had its immediate effect on the security of Dicholi and a large number of people in the town fled to Vengurla to seek protection from Mughal soldiers. A big town like Dicholi declined in population and many immigrants from this city settled at Vengurla. Thus, the immigration into the town contributed to the growth in size and population of Vengurla. Kelesi, Nagothana and Pen were the other port towns in coast region of Maharashtra which served as places for trade of European commodities. Kelesi was a good place of trading activities for European trade articles like copper and tin.[77] Nagothana and Pen had much importance as the places of trade from where Bombay had the greatest supplies of all sorts of commodities.[78] Many goods of Shivaji's territories were to be exported, from the port of Pen to Bombay.[79] Mahad seems to be a rising emporium of Maharashtra during the century. The importance of Mahad as a commercial centre increased because of its nearness to Raigad, the capital fort of Shivaji.[80] It functioned as an exchange depot between the Desh and Konkan region. It acted as commercial centre of export of foodgrains from Desh to Konkan territories.[81] Poona, Junnar, Kolhapur were the inland market towns in Maharashtra of the 17th century. Poona was an old town of a Kasba in the beginning of the 17th century.[82] But it rose to its prominence from the time when it acquired the status of the Jagir of Shahaji and Shivaji.

Though Poona remained a place of war theatre in the 17th century, it became the centre of military operation. This attracted the traders and artisans to migrate to Poona and settle there. The migration of traders in Poona town resulted in its growth in form of the establishments of new peths like Budhwar and Raviwar,[83] in the 17th century. Again this town had an advantage of being situated on the route to west Mawal and Konkan region. Moreover, Poona in the 17th century achieved its importance due to its close proximity to Shivaji's military important forts like Sinhagad and Purander.[84] Thus the political and military factors were mostly responsible for preparing the base for the growth of the urbanization of the towns like Poona during the 17th century. Junnar in the 17th century had been regarded as one of the important inland cities of Deccan.[85] The location of Junnar near the Nane pass which was one of the important trade routes between Deccan and the west coast of Maharashtra enhanced its importance as the centre of exhange of goods. In the 17th century it not only became the chief trading centre for the European goods but also acted as a collecting centre of several sorts of cloth coming from different parts of the country.[86] And with a view to purchase the cloth here at cheap rate and to sell the commercial goods coming from Arabastan, Mecca, Basra and Iran at this centre, the English East India Gompany was thinking of settling a factory at Junnar in 1675.[87]

Kolhapur in the 17th century was one of the important

markets in Shivaji's territories. The town came in possession of Shivaji in 1675.[88] It became a good trading centre for the European goods like calicoes.[89]

The political and economic policies of Shivaji were indirectly but certainly responsible for preparing the base for the growth of urbanization in Maharashtra during the 17th century. Shivaji granted the kauls of assurances to traders to continue their trade when the trade was disturbed owing to raids on peths, and ordered the thanedars of peths to employ men of Diwan for petrolling them.[90] For developing the trade of market places, he also reduced the taxes to be levied on the goods of traders. Thus, for instance, with a view of flourishing the trade of the peth of Ramnagar, Shivaji had granted the remission of Diwanhasil tax to be collected from the goods of traders in the market for twelve years.[91] He also provided guards at the chaukis established on the roads and granted security to traders. The officers, like Ghatpande, Patki, Pansare, Modvi, Metkari etc. were appointed for petrolling and keeping the trade routes on ghat safe.[92] To encourage the trade of port towns in his country, Shivaji had permitted the Portuguese, the French, the Dutch, the English to open their factories at the places like Dabhol, Rajapur, and Vengurla.[93] He also maintained friendly relations with the English and invited to trade with his ports and towns.[94] He had also ordered his soldiers not to give hindrances to the foreign merchants who had friendly relations with him.

An experience of the English merchants in this regard will illustrate this point. One of the English records refers to the fact that when one hundred oxen belonging to the English merchants were carrying the goods to Kolhapur, Shivaji with his army met them, while going against Belgaon. He not only ordered his army not to give hindrance to the English merchants but also provided protection to their goods till they reached Kolhapur.[95] With the aim of developing the trade Shivaji promised the English factors at Bombay to settle a warehouse of his merchants in Bombay for putting great quantities of goods.[96] Again, security arrangements made by

Shivaji in his towns, immediately after taking them in possession, no doubt promoted the growth of trade of towns and contributed to the urban progress in the region. Thus, when Shivaji occupied Kolhapur in 1675, posted two thousand men to guard the town and provide security to the people. He also promised the inhabitants of the town to give the good treatment.[97]

Lastly, the role of small towns known as peths or kasbas in the economy and urban growth of Maharashtra is noteworthy. They served as a link between villages and cities and helped in promoting the trade and commerce of the country and contributed to the growth of urbanization. Likewise, a large number of people in society known as Laman tribe,[98] who carried the goods from one place to another, seem to have engaged in transport industry day and night. The transport industry conducted by the Laman people was developed in this region considerably, and no doubt played a significant role in urbanization during the period under review.

Agrarian base of Urban Phenomenon in the 18th Century Maratha Country

The following discussion regarding the agricultural production of cotton, sugarcane, groundnuts, seseme etc., in the territories of Maratha country shows its relation with the growth of rural-urban centres and the economic activities of small towns such as Khed, Ranjangaon, Sangamner, Sultanpur, Nandurbar, Saswad Bhum, Shevegaon, Erandol, Edlabad, Chandwad, Pimpalner etc., during the 18th century. The towns such as Nagpur, Jalnapur, Burhanpur, Solapur, Paithan were the urban centres where the economic activities were conducted due to the growth of cotton crops in and around those places. One of the chief crops included among the agricultural produces of the adjoining territories of the above mentioned urban centres was the cotton. The value of this crop for the textile industries which thrived at those places, was indeed remarkable. The tract extending from Nagpur to Burhanpur and Paithan and its area produced a large quantity of good quality of cotton. The region of Khandesh also produced the finest variety of cotton which was exported on considerable scale to Poona and other centres of industrial activity. The abundant production of cotton in province of Solapur, and in some other parts near it, encouraged the weaving activities of the town. The cotton in those areas was produced in such large quantities that much of it was exported.[98a] The raw cotton produced in and around of Paithan encouraged the industrial activity of the town. The selling of cotton from such urban places increased enormously and resulted in the growth of export trade of cotton from Maratha country to the port of Bombay. In 1787, the English East India Company bought several bales of cloth from the urban centres in Maratha country and sold them at Bombay.[98b] The following mentioned figures would indicate the sale of bales of cloth by the English during that year.

Clothes	*No. of bales sold*
Bales of Cloth	526
Bales of Long Ells	250
Bales of Broad	030
Carpenting	040

The total quantity of bales of cloth, purchased from various towns in Maratha country and sold by the English merchants at Bombay during 1787-90, was as mentioned in table on page 150.[98c]

The sugarcane was produced on large scale in and around Indapur[98d] tract. Therefore Junnar became a prosperous market town for jaggery. Similarly, the lands in Pargana Supe[98e] and Ungirgaon[98f] produced sugarcane abundantly. So, the town of Supe served as an important

Year	*Kind of cloth*	*Quantity of Bales*	*Value in*
1784-85	Broad cloth long ells	207	10,904
1785-86	Broad cloth long ells	493	69,694
1786-87	Broad cloth long ells	679	34,702
1787-88	Broad cloth long ells	1156	60,665
1788-89	Broad cloth coarse fine super fine long ells	205	5778
1789-90	Broad cloth super fine coarse long ells	374	19,291

collecting centre of gur. The lands around the towns of Chandwad, Pimpalgaon, Basawant, Neral, produced large quantity of sugarcane and enabled them to emerge not only as collecting and distributing centres of agricultural produce but also the headquarters of pargana unit. The cultivation of sugarcane came to be concentrated in the region around the towns of Wai, and Satara also. As a result several gur making industries came to be flourished in those prants during the 18th century. The town of Satara served as important market centre for the agricultural produce and other goods. Similarly, the cultivation of groundnuts, seseme, gingely cocoanuts, produced abundantly in neighbouring provinces of Poona and Junnar,[98g] facilitated the growth of oil mill and many market centres of distribution for production in town like Poona. Indeed, Poona through its several and various trades and crafts based upon agrarian goods, came to dominate the small kasba places in western Maharashtra in the 18th century. Junnar was also well known among other towns in its prants and seem to have considerably grown as a collecting and distributing centre of agrarian produce of the villages in its unit of pargana level.

The measures undertaken by the Maratha rulers such as granting the wasteland to the farmers for bringing the land under cultivation, making availability of canal water for irrigating the lands, etc., also provided sufficient scope for the extension of cultivation and the growth of agricultural produce of the villages. The surplus produce of the land also made some of the Kasba places as the centres of agrarian goods in the neighbourhood of those villages. The towns mentioned below and situated in hinterland served as important centres of collection of agricultural produce or the market places for the products in villages around them. The table on page 107 shows the area of producing agricultural crops and the towns emerged as collecting and distributing centres of those crops during the 18th century.

Extent of Urbanization in Maratha Country during the 18th Century

Urbanization in Maharashtra in the 18th century was the outcome of different factors that helped the growth of urban centres and an urban way of life. The following discussion aims to show how the various factors directly or indirectly, separately or together, were responsible for preparing the base for the growth of urbanization in Maratha country during the 18th century.

Contemporary sources refer to more than a dozen urban centres in Maharashtra of the 18th century. Out of these Bombay[99] in 1764-65 had a population of 1 lack and 40 thousand. The population of Poona[100] city was 2 lacks in 1783-84. Therefore these two major places could be regarded as large cities in Maharashtra. Poona, in the 18th century, was the capital city of the Maratha empire and subsequently developed as a trading and administrative centre. The towns of Cheul

Kind of Crop	*The area producing agricultural crops*	*Towns emerged as collecting and distributing centres of agrarian goods*
Cotton	Tract of North Deccan, extending from Nagpur to Burhanpur, Khandesh, Paithan, Solapur	Nagpur, Jalnapur, Burhanpur, Paithan, Solapur, Erandol, Edlabad, Nandurbar, Pimpalner
Sugarcane	Villages tarfs, Haveli, Indapur, Supe, Nane Mawal, Undirgaon, Pimpalgaon, Baswant	Pune, Junnar, Satara, Supe, Chandwad, Neral
Groundnuts, Til, cocoanuts	Neral, Nane Mawal, Konkan region	Poona, Junnar, Nagar, Pen and Panvel, Kalyan, Bhiwandi
Foodgrains Rice, Jwor and Bajra	Nane Mawal, Paun Mawal, Kathapur, villages in Parganas of Wai and Shevgaon	Pune, Junnar, Wai, Nandurbar, Edlabad, Erandol, Pimpalner, Shevgaon, Sangamner, Khed, Ranjangaon, Saswad Bhum

and Rajapur were port towns and developed as commercial centres. A large number of towns like Bombay, Solapur, Yeola, Chandwad, Nagpur, Paithan, Akot, Balapur, Deulgaonraja, Khalapur, Anjangaon, Karajgaon, Jalnapur etc., developed as manufacturing centres as well as trading centres. Nagpur and Chandwad were famous places for weaving industry and the centres for manufacture of textile goods, specially fine dhotis.[101] There were other towns where the textile industries flourished well. Elichpur, Akot, and Balapur had a flourishing textile industry, which consisted of cotton cloth and carpets.[102] Khalapur,[103] Anjangaon and Jalnapur[104] were famous centres for manufacturing silk turbans. Karajgaon was a town where the craft of casting metals and manufacturing bells existed.[105] Thana, Kalyan, and Bhivandi were the centres of ship and boat building in Maharashtra during the 18th century. Yeola and Cheul were other centres of manufacturing silk.[106] Industries of silk manufacture and cotton goods and of gold thread in Yeola were the important factors responsible for its rapid growth.[107] The crafts thus attracted numerous artisans from Gujarat and the territory of the Nizam. The migration of skilled craftsmen to Yeola from adjoining territories contributed to the growth of the town. Solapur, throughout the 18th century, had a flourishing handloom industry. The industry of this town was specialised in dhotis and coloured sarees.[108] The industrial activities in the town attracted many artisans, families and trading classes to migrate from other places to that centre. Thus, the families of Khetri, Momin and Padamshalis were the immigrants who migrated from Nizam's territory to Solapur.[109] Consequently, new settlements of Peths came into being and the town grew rapidly.

Textile Industry and Paithan as a Urban Centre

Paithan was a well-known urban centre of our period and had acquired such position in relation to the textile industry that the fabrics manufactured here were in great demand and became very famous all over the country from the ancient times. Since the days of Stavahanas, Paithan was an important urban centre of textile industry and had the name for the manufacture of cotton and silk.[110] Its fame continued even in the time of Yadavas. Ibn Batuta and Marcopolo have praised the art of weaving of the skilled artisans at Paithan.[111] The weavers of Paithan were known for their art all over Maharashtra and Gujrat.[112]

During the 18th century also, Paithan enjoyed repute both for the cotton textile and silk fabrics. The manufacture of textiles was made from different kinds of fibres like cotton and silk. The textile products of Paithan included silk turbans (Pagotas or tiwats)[113], fine sarees,[114] chintz, rumals, fine dhotees[115] with brocade of silver thread, pasodi,[116] chirdi,[117] etc. Silk fabrics manufactured here included broad bordered and embroidered silk garments commonly known as *Paithani*[118] and worn by ladies, *Paithani shalu* (a cloth of fine texture), silk dhotees named as *Pitambars*.[119] The name *Paithani*[120] which has been derived from Paithan is very old going back 300-200 B.C. *Paithani* saree had a distinct style of its own in silk with elaborate gold ornamentation in palloo and border and hence it became an attraction for every bride in Maharashtra.[121] This saree was also used for giving a present by the feudal people on the occasion of the marriage.[122] Dhotees manufactured at Paithan were of two kinds i.e. the ordinary dhotees, made of cotton and another type of dhotees were the dhotees of brocade of silver thread. Yellow pitambar at Paithan was of a superior quality. The Zanana[123] pitambar was usually brocaded. The dhotees of Paithan were usually 11½ cubits long and 2½ cubits in width. A pair of ordinary dhotee was sold at prices,[124] from rupees 15 to 40, whereas a pair of silk dhotee of super quality cost any amount from rupees 60 to 70. Silk fabrics at Paithan such as fine sarees, dhotees and others met an ever growing demand in the towns like Poona and other market places in India.[125]

The turbans of Paithan were of different kinds like printed turbans of cotton cloth, known as *chiti tiwate*. A turban named *Zafarani*[126] Paithani was mostly used as presents made to important persons.

Paithani *Dupattas*[127] were cotton sheets, plain or printed, worn as wraps and were also used for garments. Ordinarily, a piece of this cloth was five to seven cubits in length and three cubits in width. Red, white, rosy, green etc. were the piece of this cloth of different varieties made at Paithan.[128] A superior quality of Dupattas made at Paithan was of fine and soft cotton sheet with silver thread work at its two ends.[129] *Pasodi*[130] *Paithani* was the thick cotton stuff and was used as rug. Chhiti Pasodi[131], Khadi Pasodi[132] etc. were the varieties of this kind of textile. Other type of textiles at Paithan such as *Mashru, Himru* and *Kinkhab* (brocade) etc., were the fabrics of fine texture used for making veils, headdresses, bridal robes and sarees.[133] *Mashru* was a kind of silk cloth, and *Himru* was a sort of embroidered cloth. *Kinkhab* manufactured at Paithan once was celebrated throughout Deccan. In 1609 a Persian ambassador who arrived at Golkonda also preferred the piece of Kinkhab of Paithan, and he took it with him at his country.[134]

The skilled artisans at Paithan were particularly specialised in production of silver and gold threads. [135] For making the silver thread, the artisans got silver by melting silver rupees. The melted silver was used into threads. The silver threads then were woven into silk cloth by using the substance made from plantains.[136]

The important raw materials required for the products of silk industry were silk and jar (silver thread). The former was imported from Yeola,[137] Bombay etc. where a considerable supply was made from Bengal, China and sometimes from Persia[138] also. The latter was brought from Sikanderabad.[139] The artisans engaged in manufacturing textiles at Paithan belonged to the communities like Koshtis,[140] Viraj[141] and Swakul Salis[142] etc.

We find that increase of demand in silk turbans in the 18th century led to occasional fall in the quality of produce. So the Maratha Government exercised supervisory control over the production process. The government ordered the manufacturers of turbans of Paithan to use silver contained Malharshahi English Surati rupees for making silver thread used for turbans. The artisans were asked to use another substance *Datyakhar* instead of plantain gum. They were instructed by state to manufacture the turbans each of 30 cubits and not of 12 or 15 cubits as before.[143] Thus for maintaining the quality control, the Maratha state exercised strict control over the artisans working in textile industry at Paithan.

The textile industry at Paithan was stimulated by various factors. Firstly, Paithan situated on the banks of river Godavari served as the principal port in the Maratha country. Ports like Broach,[144] Surat, Cambay etc., where the ships were loaded for Europe, were well joined by the land routes with the town. It also supplied the goods from Central India by the great road running through Daulatabad to Hyderabad. Thus, Paithan was well connected with the markets in India and in Europe[145] by land routes as well as by sea routes. The raw cotton, produced in and around the locality, encouraged the industrial activity. Lastly, its religious importance as a pilgrimage centre of the Hindus, Government's policy of encouraging the weaving craft, certainly promoted the growth of textile industry at Paithan.

The growing activities of textile industry stimulated the trading activity of the town also. The industry attracted the artisans making jari-gold thread to migrate to Paithan from different localities, and enabled the Muslim merchants dealing with the business to come from Surat and Burhanpur to settle in town of Paithan. This naturally helped to the growth of Paithan, in town itself. The industrial and trading activities of the town also gave rise to the wealthy[146] class of the bankers (Sahukars) like Laddu, Bakshi, Wanole, Wakhare, Baswade etc., who had a good money lending business in prosperous conditions in the town during the 18th century.[147]

It appears from the contemporary sources that the textile industry at Paithan passed through varying degree of fortunes since the last decade of the 18th century. The political uncertainty caused by the struggle for power between the Mughals, the Nizam and the Marathas and the subsequent enemy raids, had devastating effects on the industry. As a result, for want of security, the weaving communities like Viraj, Swakul Salis, in town migrated to Gujrat[148] and Poona,[149] where they were invited by the respective governments by providing them facilities in form of houses, land or money. Thus, the urban growth alongwith the textile industry of Paithan seems to have suffered a great setback at the end of the 18th century and in the beginning of the 19th century.

Poona, the capital city of the Maratha country was the chief centre of administrative and military activities. The town had a paper industry.[150] Dyeing[151] and coarse[152] cotton cloth industries also flourished in the town. A factory making ivory combs also existed in the city of Poona in the 18th century.[153] The royal factories for manufacturing cannons established in the city employed more than one hundred and fifty workers belonging to different castes and occupations.[154] Apart from this, Poona, during the Peshwa period, acted as an entrepot for the goods coming from and going to the Konkan territories and the countries above the ghats. Along with its political importance Poona became the chief military centre. As a result the number of administrative and military services increased enormously.[155] This attracted many trading classes who conducted their numerous trades in the city. The development of trade again attracted many other traders to migrate from Rajasthan, Telangana, Karnataka, Marathwada, Desh and Gujrath, Marwad etc., to settle there.[156] Among the immigrants there were artisans such as potters, leather workers, kamathis, thatchers, traders, masons, soldiers, clerks, messengers, sepoys,[157] etc. The immigrant communities[158] which migrated to Poona, were Boharas from Ahmadabad and Aurangabad, Maheshwari Baniyas from Rajasthan. Marwadi Baniyas from Jodhpur and Sirohi and Gujarati Baniyas from Gujrat. This resulted in the growth of the city in size in the form of establishment of new peths, such as Vetal, Ganesh, and Somawar[159] etc.

Again banking business in the city of Poona was in prosperous condition in the 18th century. It was stimulated and boosted because of the growing commercial activities of Poona city. And, ultimately, both contributed to the growth and development of the town. The population of the city grew so rapidly that it resulted in overcrowding of the peths.[160] Thus, the trading activities in Poona, alongwith administrative activity, contributed more to the development and growth of the city than the manufacturing activity.

Bombay was famous as a manufacturing centre of cotton and silk from the oldest times.[161] The industry of ship building developed well at this place in the 18th century.[162] It was the principal seaport of Western India through which a great volume of trade was conducted during the 18th century. It has been described as the most flourishing town in the world and grand storehouse of all Arabian and Persian commerce.[163] It had cotton trade relations with China. These trade relations resulted in the shift of cotton trade centre from Surat to Bombay. By this change Bombay emerged as the entrepot of cotton trade in place of Surat and became the leading city of Western India. This made Bombay overcrowded with merchants, bankers and working people who migrated from Surat and other parts of Gujrat. The growth of Bombay city in the 18th century depended on many and various factors. Its trade with principal seaports of India and other countries and interior towns brought it prosperity. Besides, for the development of this port the availability of better shipping facilities, excellent docks, good arrangement for repairing ships etc., all these factors also played a vital role in bringing about the expansion and development of the trade of the city. The waterways of Bombay were also important for its international commercial development. Again the custom duty that was levied on all import-export goods varied from two to five per cent,[164] and sometimes it was reduced or was abolished by the British Government.[165] This also helped to stimulate the growth of the trade of Bombay and prosperity of the city.

Other towns like Junnar, Pen and Panvel also developed as commercial centres owing to their location on the trade routes. The location of Junnar near the Nane pass which was one of the highways of trade between the Deccan and the west coast of Maharashtra contributed to its rise to prominence. Therefore, Junnar played an important role in inter-provincial trade. Pen and Panvel were important ports in prant of Kalyan Bhivandi. They were good centres of exports and imports.[166] Pen was the centre of considerable traffic between Deccan and sea coast.[167] Its communication with Bombay and Deccan by the Bor pass made the port an important trading centre. Panvel was a centre of trade between Poona and Bombay.[168] It rose to importance along with Bombay as the direct route from Bombay to Deccan lies through it. Pandharpur was a famous place of pilgrimage of Hindus and also a trade centre of the 18th century. It had a good market which supplied locally produced goods such as grains, cloth etc. It served as an emporium for the various foreign commodities especially of the English imported to the centre through Bombay and Poona.[169] Its religious importance attracted a large number of people to the town and, naturally, contributed to its growth of population.

There can be no exaggeration in saying that the mints established by the Peshwa at places like Poona,[170] Daulatabad, Nagothan,[171] Chandwad etc., would have indirectly helped in the development and growth of urbanization in the region. Again Kasbas or Peths which were the market places and manufacturing centres for the village people served as a link between the villages and cities and thus played an important role in the process of urbanization in Maharashtra.[172]

Transport industry was well developed in Maharashtra in the 18th century. The tribes like Laman Banjaras, Naiks and Charans etc., followed the profession of carrying the goods from one place to another. They brought the goods from Bombay and Pen to Poona and Satara.[173] They also loaded the goods from long distances like Surat in Gujarat and unloaded them at Nasik, Poona and Nandurbar. Thus the transport industry no doubt contributed to the growth of urbanization in Maharashtra. Lastly, the economic policy of the Maratha rulers cannot be ignored for the urban progress in the province of Maharashtra. The communication facilities provided with dharmashalas[174] (rest-house), wells[175] for drinking water and measures undertaken by the rulers for securing the roads of trade etc., all these together certainly created a favourable situation for promoting urban growth in Maharashtra during the 18th century.

From the above discussion, it appears that the political, administrative, economic, geographical and religious factors helped in bringing of the urban growth and development in Maratha country in the 17th and the 18th centuries.

References and Footnotes

1. This can be seen in the following research papers: Urbanization in Maharashtra during the 17th century contributed by the author in Sanshodhak, the periodical of Itihasacharya V.K. Rajwade, Mandal, Dhulia, March, 1985, pp. 38-48;
Urbanization in Maharashtra in the 18th century, by the same author contributed to the proceedings of Indian History Cogresses, Burdwan Session, 1983, pp. 478-483; also see Growth of a Market Economy of Towns in the 18th century Maharashtra by the same author, paper presented at the 47th session of IHC at Srinagar, Oct. 1986.

1a. V.V. Joshi, Rajdhani Raigad.

2. Awalaskar, S.V., Raigadchi Jiwankatha, p. 4.

3. Ibid., p. 5.

4. Book of Bombay by James Doughlas, p. 409 quoted from Awalaskar's op. cit., p. 26.

5. Rao, Studies in Indian History (ed.), "Rajgad the first Capital of Shivaji" by A.R. Kulkarni, pp. 168-169.

6. V.D. Rao, op. cit., p. 169.

7. Ibid., p. 168 and pp. 170-171.

8. M.S. Mate, Maratha Architecture, p. 69.

9. Kamal Gokhale, Shivputra Sambhaji, p. 425.

10. Grant Duff, History of the Marathas, p. 200.

11. Shivkalin Patrasar Sangraha (PSS) letter 1053.

12. Mate, M.S. op. cit., p. 65.

13. Saryu Doshi, Shivaji and Facets of Maratha Culture (ed.), p. 40.
14. Ibid., p. 39.
15. Mate, M.S., op. cit., p. 65.
16. Apte B.K., A History of the Maratha Navy and Merchant Ships, p. 15.
17. Mate, op. cit., p. 65; also see Apte, B.K., op. cit., p. 21.
18. Awalaskar, S.V. op. cit., p. 57.
19. Ibid., p. 167.
20. Shree Sampradayachi Kagad Patre, Letter No. 11.
21. Shivcharitra Sahitya, IV, 733.
22. Sambhajikalin Patrasar Sangraha, letter No. 235.
23. Ibid., letters 186 & 252.
24. PSS, letter 279.
25. Itihas Manjiri, ed. by Apte, D.V., pp. 95-97.
26. Sambhajikalin Patrasar Sangraha (SKPSS) letter nos. 13, 15, 16.
27. Ibid., letter No. 88.
28. Ibid., letter No. 93.
29. SCS, 3, letter Nos. 509, 515, 517, 523, 524; also see MIS by V.K. Rajwade-XV-128-76. SKPSS, letter No. 16, 93.
30. SKPSS letter No. 13.
31. Ibid., letter No. 67.
32. Shree Sampradayachi Kagadpatre, letter No. 10.
33. Shiv Charitra Sahitya, IV, letters 733-41.
34. Mali. M.G., Shree Mouni Maharaj, p.21.
35. Marathyanchya Itihasachi Sadhane (MIS) by V.K. Rajwade, XX, letter No. 217.
36. P.M. Joshi and Sherwani, History of Medieval Deccan, p. 16.
37. SPSS, II, 1421.
38. Kulkarni, A.R., Maharashtra in the Age of Shivaji, Poona, 1967.
39. Shivakalin Patrasar Sangraha: Part I, letter No. 1019 hereafter referred to as SPSS.
40. Guha, J.P., The Voyages of Thevenot and Careri, (1982), p. 221.
41. Kulkarni, A.R., Maharashtra in the Age of Shivaji (1967), p. 219.
42. English Records on Shivaji, by Paranjape, B.G. and Kale, D.V., Shiva Charitra Karyalaya, Poona (1931), Vol. II, 214 hereafter referred to as ERS; also see B.G. Tamaskar's Life and Work of Malik Ambar, 1978, p. 355.
43. ERS, II, 214.
44. Pissurlekar, P.S., Portuguese-Marathe Sambandh (In Marathi) May, 1967, p. 41.

45. Shivashahi Portuguese Kagadpatre, S.S. Desai (editor), letter No. 2, p. 4.
46. Portuguese-Marathe Sambandh, p. 43.
47. Tamaskar, Life and Work of Malik Ambar, p. 355.
48. Kulaba District Gazetteer, p. 733.
49. Shiv Charitra Sahitya, Part 10, letter No. 22.
50. Fryer, Vol. I, pp. 193-99, Abbe Carre, p. 191, quoted from Maharashtra in the Age of Shivaji, p. 219.
51. Guha, J.P., India in the Seventeenth Century, Vol. II i.e. the Voyages of Thevenot and Careri, (1982), p. 140.
52. SPSS, II, letter No. 1536, p. 442.
53. Sen, S.N., Foreign Biographies of Shivaji, p. 50.
54. Shiva Charitra Shitya, Part 10, letter No. 22 and 6.
55. ERS, Part I, p. 128.
56. Shivashahi Portuguese Kagadpatre, letter No. 17.
57. Sabhasad Bakhar, p. 97.
58. The Voyages of Thevenot and Careri ed. by Guha, p. 22.
59. Ratnagiri District Gazetteer, p. 749.
60. SPSS, II, letter No. 1689.
61. SPSS, I, letter No. 918, p. 222.
62. Sabhasad Bakhar, p. 97 and also see Dr. Balkrishna's Shivaji The Great, Vol. IV, p. 151.
63. Sen, S.N., Foreign Biographies of Shivaji, p. 179.
64. SPSS, II, letter No. 1563.
65. Ratnagiri District Gazetteer, p. 786.
66. SPSS, I, letter No. 886, and also see ERS, I, 352.
67. SPSS, I, letter No. 886, SPSS, II, letter Nos. 1748, 1885.
68. ERS, I, 352.
69. ERS, I, p. 16.
70. Ratnagiri District Gazetteer, p. 812.
71. Shivashahi Portuguese Kagadpatre, letter Nos. 62 and 63.
72. Ibid., letter no. 48.
73. Ratnagiri District Gazetteer, p. 812.
74. Shivashahi Portuguese Kagadpatre, letter No. 79, p. 81.
75. Maharashtra in the Age of Shivaji, p. 239.
76. Portuguese-Marathe Sambandh, pp. 117-118; also see History of Aurangzeb, J.N. Sarkar, Vol. IV, p. 243.
77. ERS, I, p. 315.
78. ERS, I, 410, p. 802, ERS, II, p. 305.

79. ERS, I, p. 77.
80. Kulaba District Gazetteer, p. 852.
81. Apte, B.K., The Maratha Navy and Merchant Ship (1973), p. 68.
82. Gadgil, Poona, A Socio-economic Survey, Part II, (1952), p. 3.
83. Ibid., p. 5.
84. Ibid., p. 6.
85. ERS, I, p. 316.
86. ERS, II, p. 105.
87. Ibid., and also see Shivakalin Patrasar Sangraha, II, letter No. 1528.
88. ERS, II, p. 41.
89. ERS, II, p. 108.
90. SCS, II, letter No. 358 and SPSS, I, letter No. 1285.
91. SPSS, II,letter No. 1777.
92. Ibid., III, letter No. 2599.
93. Portuguese-Marathe Sambandh by Pisurlekar, p. 74; also see SPSS, II, letter No. 1590.
94. ERS, I, 347, 350, 352 and 429 and also ERS, II, 46; also see SPSS, II, letter No. 2086, p. 626.
95. ERS, II, 198.
96. ERS, I, 429.
97. ERS, II, p. 62.
98. SPSS, I, letter No. 1048, p. 284.

98a. Gazetteer of Bombay Presidency, Vol. XX, p. 264.

98b. From Commercial Department letters from the Honourable Court of Directors, Vol. I, 1787-90, p. 11.

98c. Reports of the Select Committee appointed by the Court of Directors of East India Company, p. 6.

98d. Peshwa Diaries, I, Sanads, 287 and 289.

98e. Ibid., VI, p. 254.

98f. Ibid., VI, Sanad, 711.

98g. Ibid., VI, Sanad, 289.

99. Gazetteer of Bombay city, I, p. 155.
100. Grewal, J.S. and Indu Banga, Studies in Urban History, p. 98.
101. Bhave, V.K., Peshwekalin Maharashtra, p. 341.
102. Ibid., p. 253.
103. Ibid.
104. Peshwa Diaries, VIII, Sanad 1076.
105. Bhave, V.K., op. cit., p. 253.

106. Gazetteer of Bombay Presidency, XVI, p. 155.
107. Ibid., pp. 662-63.
108. Bhave, V.K., op. cit., p. 341.
109. Kakade, R.G., Socio-economic Survey of Weaving Communities in Solapur, p. 13.
110. Das, Economic, History of Deccan, p. 143.
111. Marcopolo Part II, p. 391.
112. Panse, M.G., Yadav Kalın Maharashtra, p. 215.
113. Peshwa Diaries, VI, Sanad 566; also see Peshwaichya Sawalit, by N.G. Chapekar, Introduction, p. 58.
114. Peshwa Daftar, edited by G.S. Sardesai, (hereafter referred to as PD, Vol. 22, letter No. 53; also see Bhave, V.K., Peshwekalin Maharashtra, p. 264.
115. Peshwa Diaries, VII, Sanad 716, p. 290.
116. V.K. Bhave, op. cit., p. 268.
117. This kind of cloth was a sort of garment used for little girls; see V.K. Bhave, op. cit., p. 268.
118. PD, Vol. 32, letter No. 9.
119. V.K. Bhave, op. cit., p. 272.
120. Gazetteer of India, Maharashtra State, Aurangabad District, p. 472.
121. Ibid.
122. PD, Part 32, letter No. 9.
123. Gazetteer of India, Maharashtra State, Aurangabad District, p. 471.
124. V K. Bhave, op. cit., p. 268.
125. PD, Part 32, letter nos. 9, 94, 95, 97,99, 100, 101, 103.
126. N.G. Chapekar, op. cit., (Introduction), p. 58; also see Peshwa Diaries, VI, Sanad 566.
127. PD, Vol. 22, letter No. 53.
128. Ibid., Vol. 32, letter No. 97.
129. PD, Part 32, letter No. 103.
130. Ibid., Part 22, letter No. 66.
131. Ibid., letter No. 100.
132. Ibid, letter No. 103.
133. S.H. Bilgrami, and M.C. Wilmot, Historical and Descriptive sketches of His Highness the Nizam's Dominion, Bombay, 1883, pp. 416-422.

134. Gazetteer of India, Maharashtra State, Aurangabad District, p. 469.
135. Peshwa Diaries, VIII, Sanad 1077.
136. Ibid., Sanads 1086-77.
137. Gazetteer of India, Maharashtra State, Aurangabad District, p 472.
138. T.T. Mahajan, Industry, Trade and Commerce during the Peshwa Period, (Jaipur, 1989), p. 17.
139. Gazetteer of India, Aurangabad District, p. 466.
140. Ibid.
141. Joshi, S G., Marathwada Sanshodhan Mandal, Varshik (In Marathi), (1975), p. 7.
142. J.S. Grewal and Indu Banga, Studies in Urban History, p. 100.
143. Peshwa Diaries, VIII, Sanads 1076 and 1077.
144. H.G. Rawlinson, Intercourse between India and Western World, (Cambridge), 1926, 119.
145. Ibid., p. 109.
146. S.G. Joshi, op. cit., p. 6.
147. N.G. Chapekar, op. cit., p. 134; also see Shivaji and Facets of Maratha Culture, edited by Doshi, p. 113.
148. S.G. Joshi, op. cit., p. 7.
149. J.S. Grewal and Indu Banga, op. cit., p. 101.
150. V.D. Divekar, Political factor in the rise and decline of "Cities in Pre-British India", Studies in Urban History, (ed.) Grewal and Indu Banga.
151. Diaries, VII, pp. 108-109.
152. Gadgil, D.R., Poona, A Socio-economic Survey, I, p. 103.
153. Gazetteer of Bombay Presidency, XVIII, Part II, p. 201.
154. Peshwekalin Maharashtra, p. 426.
155. Gadgil, D.R., Poona, A Socio-economic Survey, Part II, p. 35.
156. Ibid., p. 99.
157. J.S. Grewal and Indu Banga, op. cit., p. 99.
158. Ibid., p. 100.
159. Poona, A Socio-economic Survey, Part II, p. 7,
160. Diaries, VIII, Sanad 1154.
161. The Gazetteer of Bombay City and Island, I, p. 462.
162. Agaskar, M.S., "Early History of Bombay Docks and Ship building", Potdar Commemoration Volume, p. 333.

163. Ives' Voyage in Bombay quoted from Indian Society in the 18th century, pp. 351-52, from Minutes of Evidences taken before the committee of the whole house and the select committee on the affairs of East India Company, p. 257.
164. Gazetteer of Bombay Presidency, Vols. IX and X, Part III, p. 33.
165. Gazetteer of Bombay City and Island, II, p. 447.
166. Ibid., Vol. II, p. 446.
167. Diaries, VII, Sanad 474.
168. Maharashtra State Gazetteer, Kulaba District, p. 915.
169. Ibid., p. 911.
170. Gazetteer of the Bombay Presidency, XX, p. 292.
171. Peshwekalin Maharashtra, p. 404.
172. Diaries, II, Sanad 245.
173. Diaries, VIII, Sanad 1076.
174. Diaries, VII, Sanad 702.
175. Peshwekalin Maharashtra, pp. 41-42.

5

Social Barriers and Communal Harmony between the Hindus and the Muslims in Maratha Country

While studying the contemporary records, we find that there were some sources which caused the social bitterness to the people in the Maratha country. But, at the same time, one can realise the fact that the factors which brought about the socio-cultural harmony between the Hindus and the Muslims, had a great impact on the society in medieval Maharashtra.

Social Barriers

The caste system which was predominant in Hindu society of Maratha country guided the social intercourse between the Hindus and the Muslims and acted as a social barrier between both the communities. The Marathas who treated the Muslims socially outsiders called them Yawan[1] and observed the social taboos in different fields of life.

As between various castes of Hindus, there was no interdining between the Hindus and the Muslims in Maratha country of medieval period. Dining with the Muslim was supposed to pollute the Hindu religion and therefore taking food with the Muslim was prohibited. Once, the Brahmins of Paithan dined with a Mohamedan person and so they had to undergo the penance. The persons who disobeyed to undergo the penance were punished by the Maratha Government by confiscating their inamlands.[2] The regulations framed by the Peshwas concerning the entrance in the temple of Pandurang at Pandharpur clearly indicate that the Muslims were not allowed to enter the Hindu shrines at the holy places.[3] Similarly, marriage taboos were also strictly observed in Hindu society of Maratha country.

Mixed marriages between Hindus and Muslims usually did not take place. And even if they were performed they had serious practical consequences. For instance, though the Peshwa Bajirao I was attached to a Mohamedan mistress Mastani, the Hindu society did not bear the attachment of a Muslim lady to a Hindu person and treated her badly. The relatives of the Peshwa also pressed him to renounce all the attachment towards this lady and ultimately seized her and kept in confinement in palace of Shaniwarwada.[4] Likewise, a Kazi, who performed the marriage between the daughter of a Muslim slave and a Hindu dyer in Poona was finally punished by the Government by confiscating his Watan Inam and the right of levying taxes from the Muslims in town.[5] Even the social intercourse i.e., living together in one locality was also not observed between the Hindus and the Muslims. For instance, the Muslim weaving communities in Poona town resided in Gunj ward and the Hindu weavers lived in other wards of the town.[6] Likewise, the Muslim weavers in Solapur town in the 18th century lived in Shukrawar and Shaniwar wards whereas the Hindu weavers such as Niralis, Lingayat, non-Lingayat, Koshtis etc., lived in another part of the town.[7] There seems to be no transfusion of skills and techniques between the weaving artisans of both the communities.[7a]

The source of tension between both the communities was the fear of Hindus of the pollution of their religion by the members of Muslim community. Thus, the Muslim officer namely Saiyad Pirjada brought obstacles in the sacrifices performed by the Hindu people in Mauja Mankeshwar of Bhoom pargana. He threw bones in the midst of Brahmins while dining and touched and polluted the Brahmin women. He also did other acts such as opening liquor distilleries, removing stones from Hindu temples[8] etc., and tried to humiliate the religious feelings of Hindus. Another Muslim officer namely Sidi Sat of Anjanwel, one of the Governors of Sidi Yakut of Janjira, committed outrage on the temple of Parsram, the holy shrine of the Peshwas in Konkan region.[9]

Another reason for the social tension between both the communities was desecration of Hindu temples and religious faiths by the Muslims. Afzalkhan, the Bijapuri Sardar, committed acts of vandalism such as desecrating the Hindu shrines of Vithoba at Pandharpur and of Bhavani at Tuljapur.[10] This humiliated the religious faiths of the Marathas. Aurangzeb had appointed a special officer to supervise the destruction of Hindu temples in Maharashtra.[11] In 1693 the Mughal emperor had ordered to demolish the temples near Sheogaon. Again Muslims destroyed the Hindu temples and built the Muslim tomb[12] or mosques in those places. So did the Marathas vice-versa. For instance, a Hindu shrine of a god Shri Sunder Narayan at Nasik was demolished by the Muslims during the Mughal regime and a mosque was built in its place. So during the regime of Peshwas the same mosque was excavated by the Marathas and a Hindu temple was built in its place.[13]

Other reason for the Hindu-Muslim tension was forcefully conversions of the Hindus made by the Muslim rulers. Bajaji Nimbalkar and Netaji Palkar, the famous Maratha chiefs were forcefully converted to Islam by the Muslim rulers.[14] In 1680 A.D., Isthamkhan, the officer of Aurangzeb forcefully converted thirty-five men, women and children in Yaval village and the prayer was taught to them.[15] In 1700, two Maratha Sardars namely Khanderao and Jagjivanrao Gujar were converted to Islam.[16]

Thus, there are many instances of individual and mass conversions of Hindus during the reign of Aurangzeb. Similarly, the Kulkarni of the Harsul, who was Brahmin by caste, was forcefully converted to Muslim during the regime of King Sambhaji who later on reconverted him to Hinduism.[17] These acts of forced conversions certainly produced a sense of resentment among the Marathas and created the hostilities between both the communities for many times.

Social assimilation of Hindu-Muslim Communities

It is also not equally true that all the Hindus and the Muslims in Maratha country were total aliens in all the matters. The Maratha rulers had employed a number of Muslim persons in State's services[18] and obtained valuable co-operation from them for conducting the administration. Thus, King Shivaji employed the Muslim men such as Rustom-i-Jama-II, Siddi Fatehkhan, Siddi Hilal, Ibrahim Khan, Munshi Haidar, Madari Mehtar, Daulatkhan and seven hundred other Pathans[19] in his State services. The King Sambhaji also employed the Muslim servants like Kaviji Muhammad, Siddi Mistry, Daulatkhan and others.[20] He had also appointed the Muslim person like Shaikh Muhammad to the post of a Diwan of Supe Prant.[21]

The Maratha kings also played an important role in fostering of religious toleration in Hindu-Muslim communities in their kingdom. Shivaji contributed largely to the social and cultural harmony among the Hindus and the Muslims. The King Shivaji went on visit to the Muslim saints such as Baba Yakuti of Kelashi frequently. He gave him equal respect which he paid to his guru, saint Ramdas. He sought his blessings on many occasions. Several other Maratha sardars also paid him visit and worshipped the Muslim saint. This attitude of Maratha king contributed to develop the religious contact between the Hindus and the Muslims of those times. The King Shivaji by making rise above the social barriers and taboos of religious faith, developed the religious attitude of his subjects towards the toleration. Similarly, the Maratha kings and their nobles largely contributed towards Hindu-Muslim unity in the society of their age by granting the lands and allowances to the Muslim persons, the mosques, dargas and pirs. Shivaji had made the grants to the tombs of Muslim saints. He issued the grants to Baba Yakuti of Kelashi.[22] The King also gave the grants in form of Inam lands to the Muslims. The Muslim faqir of Gove in Wai Pargana was granted some Inam land by the King. Shivaji also continued the Inam lands to the Muslim pirs of Sayeed Hazarat Pir Hasan Khatal and Qazi Qasim Pirzade in Pune Pargana.[23] Likewise, his son Chhatrapati Sambhaji had sanctioned the yearly grant of one hundred hons to meet the expenses of lamp, sweeper and offerings to the pir of Sayyid Abdulla Khan of Fort Fonda.[24] Surabkhan at Varali was granted one Charar of land of mauje Dharmapur by the King Sambhaji.[25] He also granted the Inam village and Inam lands of mauje Kotigera, Kazipura, Yetmadpur, to Sayed Adam Karim.[26] There is no doubt that the royal grants made by the Maratha kings to the Muslim saints and persons, were the acts of their charity for feeding the poor and pious men in the society, but they also served as a medium of contact between the kings and their Muslim subjects. This finally helped to bring about the communal harmony between two groups of Hindu-Muslim population in the Maratha country.

It is but natural that when these two communities came closer or lived together they forgot the differences between them and also left their isolated life caused due to the socio-religious taboos.

Muslim Saints and Hindu-Muslim Unity

Muslim saints had a number of Hindu followers. Such Hindus in Maratha country also devoted their whole life for worshipping the Dargas of the Muslim saints. The Hindumen in medieval Maharashtra alike the Muslims also participated in the celebrations of Muharram, Urs and Bara Imam[27] joyfully. Not only the families of Maratha sardars like Maloji Bhosle, but also the common masses very often gave visit to the shrines of Muslim saints like Shah Sharif, Abdur Rahman Chisti and such others. The Muslim saint namely Shaikh Muhammad had acquired a full hearted respect and honour from the Muslims as well as from the Hindus in those days.[28] In fact the Muslim saints, or pirs were a kind of medium through which the atmosphere for gradual understanding of amity and unity between both the communities was created. Thus, the Muslim saints paved the way leading towards the communal harmony among the Hindus and the Muslims in Maratha country.

Social gap betwen upper group of nobles was much less than in other groups in Hindu-Muslim society. That is why a Muslim nobleman when offered a feast to a invited guest of the noble group did not feel a sense of inferiority while observing the Hindu social and food taboos. For example, when Peshwa Bajirao I with Maratha troops met the Nizam near Udgir in 1732, the latter honoured the Marathas by giving them cloths of honour and offered them sweetmeals and thus kept social distance within the limitations by observing Hindu food taboos.[29]

Cultural Unity between the Hindus and the Muslims

Some factors which were social and economic in nature were mostly responsible for bringing about the cultural unity between both the communities. They enabled them to help each other during the hard times. The common problems like famine or the raids of enemy's army on the villages devastated the human life. During the course of such calamities the Hindus as well as the Muslims had to face the problems of food scarcity and shelter. As a result social contacts of the relations of amity and the unity between both the communities were developed considerably. They took part in one another's ceremonies of joys or sorrowful incidents. This ultimately contributed to the development of the synthesis of socio-religious practices of the Hindus and Muslims. Therefore, one can find a remarkable common life, social and cultural in its nature, of the Hindu-Muslim communities in the Maratha country.

The Marathas participated in Muslim festivals and shared the joys of the Muslims. Many of them adopted the life of Fakir in the month of Muharram[30] while others shared the joys by paying the grant of allowances to Muslim pir. The Peshwa Madhavrao I made the cash allowance to Shekh Sadat[31] Pir on occasion of Muharram festival in Poona in 1765. Other people in villages also distributed the cash among the Muslim fakirs on occasion of Muslim fairs.[32] Thus, by adopting the practice of granting lands and allowances to the Muslim Pirs, the Marathas not only participated in their festivals, but also won the respect and confidence of the Muslim population in the society. The Maratha who came into direct contact with the Muslim people, were considerably Influenced by Muslim customs and religious beliefs and socially this led to foster the religious toleration in rural society of the Marathas.

The participation of the Marathas in Muslim festivals provided them an opportunity of sharing the joys of the Muslim community. Usually the Muslim fairs were attended both by Muslims and Marathas. Thus, when annual fair was held at Kasba Jainapur in honour of Pir Najuk Saheb both the communities attended it and shared the joys.[33] Similarly the Hindus always went to visit the Muslim saints alongwith the presents and gifts on many occasions. Shivaji paid visits to Baba Yakuti[34] of Kelashi, to Moni Bawa[35] at Pedgaon for their blessings. Therefore, there is nothing surprising if the Maratha women worshipped Muslim Pir and offered eatable to it. Once, Kashibai the wife of Peshwa Bajirao I had offered food to Pir Shekh Salla in order to fulfil the vow which she had taken earlier.[36] Again like Hindu saints, the Muslim saints were provided with Khairat i.e., food consisting of grain rice, gram etc., by the Maratha people in the village.[37] It is thus obvious that in providing food to Muslim Fakirs no food taboos were observed and the Muslim Mulla, Kazi, Pir, Fakir had become the parts of Maratha society.[38] Like the Marathas, a few Muslims also participated in Hindu festivals. They would join the Hindu festivals like Dassara, Divali, and shared the joys together. For example, Mastani, wife of Peshwa Bajirao I, used to sing the songs and make the dances on anniversary celebration day of Hindu god of Krishna and also on occasion of Ganpati festival in Peshwa's palace at Poona.[39] Other Muslims participated in Hindu festivals of Dasara and Divali by presenting Nazars to them.

Thus, Daji Abdulla, Pir Khan, Pahad Khan,[40] Mr. Mustafakhan, Mirza Kasab Beg[41] and such other Muslim persons had opportunities of sharing the joys of Hindus on the occasion of the festival of Dasara by sending them presents. The Maratha women were also honoured by the Muslims. Sidi Yakut gave honour to the wife of Peshwa Madhavrao I, when she visited the holy place of Hindu deity at Hareshwar[42] in his territory.

The above description giving two different types of social picture of Hindu-Muslim communities in Maratha society leads us to conclude that though there were social barriers in Hindu society, the social contacts between the Hindus and the Muslims were well developed. The lower group of castes in Hindu society in Maharashtra irrespective of religion, interdining and intermarriages had a large number of avenues for social intercourse with the Muslims. The Maratha noble class or royal families had less opportunity for mixing socially with the Muslim feudal classes of those times. Moreover, social taboos were much less in villages than in Maratha country.

References and Footnotes

1. Peshwa Diaries, VIII, S. 1136; also see Peshewkalin Maharashtra by V.K. Bhave, p. 211.
2. Ibid., VIII, S. 1136.
3. Ibid., VIII, S. 1129.
4. Sinha, H.N., Rise of Peshwas, p. 200.
5. Peshwa Diaries, VIII, S. 1116.
6. Gadgil, D.R., Poona, A Socio-economic Survey, Part II, p. 8 and also see Studies in Urban History, edited by Grewal and Indu Banga, p. 100.

7. Kakade, R.G., A Socio-economic Survey of Weaving Communities in Solapur, p. 13.

7a. Grewal and Indu Banga, op. cit., p. 103.

8. Peshwa Diaries, VIII, S. 1007.

9. Parashis, Life of Brahmendra Swami (Marathi), p. 43.

10. Kulkarni, V.B. Shivaji the Portrait of Patriot, p. 54.

11. Sharma, R.S., Religious Policy of the Mughal Emperors, p. 34.

12. Ibid., p. 147.

13. Shiva Charitra Sahitya, Part 2, Lekh no. 314.

14. Pagadi Setu Madhavrao, Chhatrapati Shivaji, p. 189.

15. Kulkarni, G.T., The Mughal-Maratha Relations, p. 20.

16. Ibid., p. 21.

17. Bendre, Maharashtra Itihasachi Sadhaned, Part II, no. 169, pp. 199-200.

18. Sarkar, J.N., Shivaji and his Times, p. 250, Shivakalin Patrasar Sangraha, letter no. 1300, Sabhasad Bakhar, p. 54.

19. Shejwalkar, T.S., Shri Shiva Chhattrapati, pp. 360, 375, Sabhasad Bakhar, p. 51, Shivadigvijaya Bakhar, pp. 123-128.

20. Joshi, P.S., Chhatrapati Sambhaji, p. 304.

21. SKPSS, letter no. 225.

22. Sarkar, J.N., SHT, p. 368.

23. Sanads and Letters, p. 121.

24. SCS, VIII, 46, p. 51.

25. SKPSS, letter no. 206.

26. Ibid., Letter nos. 237 and 238.

27. Sherwani, H.K., "Cultural Influences under Ahmad Shah Wali Bahmani". Islamic Culture, Vol. XVIII, 1944, p. 3 5, quoted in *Cultural Archaeology of Ahmadnagar*, by P.G. Gadre, pp. 197-198

28. Gadre, P.G., Cultural Archaeology, p. 198.

29. Aitihasik Sankirna Sahitya Khand 6, (1946) *BISM Quarterly* series no. 64, letter no. 10, pp. 11-13.

30. Peshwa Diaries, VII, S. 685.

31. Ibid.

32. Ibid., 650.

33. Ibid.

34. Shiv Digvijaya Bakhar, pp. 91-92, Ekyanva Kalmi Bakhar, p. 136.

35. SCS, Khand 4, Lekh 733 and 735.

36. Selection from Peshwa Daftar (ed. by G.S. Sardesai), Part 43, p. 91.
37. Aitihasic Sankirna Sahitya, Part 14, BISM Quarterly Series no 106, (1973), pp. 62-67.
38. Setu Madhavrao Pagadi, op. cit.
39. Sharda Deshmukh, Shiv Kalatil va Peshwakalatil Shree Jiwan, p. 121.
40. Peshwa Diaries, VII, S. 774.
41. Ibid., VIII, S. 1150.
42. Aitihasik Sankirna Sahitya, VI, BISM Quarterly series no. 64, p. 73.

6

Social and Occupational Groups in Urban Society of Maratha Country

Urban Social Groups

Several towns in Maharashtra such as Poona, Satara, Faltan, Mudhol, Talegaon, Wai, Cheul, Rajapur, Solapur, Jalanapur, Yeola, Pandharpur, Nasik, Saswad, Supe Khed etc., represent the different categories of towns like, capital place, port towns, industrial towns, religious centres and small market towns (Kasbas) etc. The picture emerging from contemporary sources reveals that the population in the above urban places in Maratha country of the 18th century seems to have divided in the following groups: (1) Maratha nobles and government officials (2) Commercial groups (3) Professional or occupational groups (4) Labourers.

1. *Maratha nobles*: The important group in capital as well as other towns like Satara, Wai, Sangli, Nasik, Talegaon, Mudhol, Faltan etc., was the nobility. This can be corroborated with the evidence of Charles Warre Malet, the British resident at Peshwa's court who says that he visited many houses of several Maratha noblemen in town of Poona.[1] Poona, being the administrative centre and capital place of Maratha country

the nobles had their own camp and camping sites in the town.[2] The Maratha nobles like Balajipant Damale, Balaji Naik Baramatikar, Patvardhan, Ghorpade, Dabhade of Talegaon, Raste Shinde Holkar etc, naturally built palaces in towns.[3] It is true that they did not form the majority of the people in urban places but they were most significant group and occupied high position in urban society of those times. The main source of income of this group in town was the jagir (or Saranjam) of territory assigned them by the Peshwas.[4] Thus, Govind Hari Patvardhan, one of the Maratha nobles, at Miraj held a military Saranjam of Rs. 22,50,000 and also received the revenues from the mahals in his jagir.[5] Likewise, Murar Rao Ghorpade of Mudhol, Piraji Naik Nimbalkar of Faltan, received the territories yielding an income of Rs. 500,000 and Rs. 15,00,000 respectively.[6] Some of the nobles also possessed the right of minting coins. The mints established by the nobles also became a source of their income.[7] Sardars like Dabhade also enjoyed the rights of Sardeshmukhi, Sardeshkulkarni, etc.,[8] and also received the income from custom duties levied at custom places established at passes and on the roads.[9] The Brahmin nobles like Balaji pant Thosar too, enjoyed the position of power among the Maratha nobles.[10] A few of them had established matrimonial relations with the Peshwas.[11] And along with the wealth and power, they also enjoyed a position of respect among the urban social groups. But it is also surprising to learn that many of the Maratha nobles borrowed the money from the bankers in town[12] and they were in debt to the latter.

Another social group of inhabitants in towns was of the government officials associated with the administrative works of Maratha state. They were the Deshmukhs,[13] Kamavisdars,[14] Deshpandes,[15] Jamidars,[16] Faujdars,[17] Kotwals,[18] Judges,[19] Clerks, Shete-Mahajans,[20] Chaudhari, Awati, Dange, Pathaki,[21] and Priest.[22] They can be conveniently grouped in following categories relating to various departments like revenue, military, judicial, commercial and office of priest. Deshmukhs, Deshpandes were the hereditary officials in town,[23] and worked in connection with land revenue, watans, inams,[24] and administrative jobs of pargana. Hence they commanded the power and prestige in the urban society. Deshmukhs belonged to Maratha caste whereas Deshpandes, Desais were the Brahmins.[25] While other officials in port towns belonged to such other communities like Panchakalashi, Mali and Muslim[26] etc. Shete-Mahajans who were the heads of Kasba and were responsible for its growth,[27] were the members of both the Gotsabhas (judicial bodies) of Pargana and of Kasba. The association of these members with the administration of justice and trade certainly helped them to enjoy the position of great respect among other groups in towns. It is worth noting here that Shete-Mahajans belonged to different castes such as Shimpi[28] (tailor), Maratha,[29] Brahmin,[30] Baniyas, Jains[31] and so on. Shete-Mahajans possessed the power and prestige in urban society of our period. They were distinguished officials from bankers, traders and potadars in market towns. The Peshwa government used to grant them land as rewards. The word "Pattan Sethi" was applied only to the Shetes of big towns.[32] The Shetes were honoured by the government by giving them clothes of honour.[33]

Other social group in towns was the commercial group. A large number of people engaged in crafts and trades thus formed the basis of the social pyramid of Poona town in the 18th century. This group was composed of traders, bankers, artisans, craftsmen, brokers etc. Special amenities offered by the government to the members of this group was a dominant factor which attracted them to the town.[34] Thus, Boharas, Gujarathi Baniyas, Marwadi Baniyas, Maheshwari Baniyas were the noteworthy communities among immigrant traders in Poona in the 18th century. Among skilled artisans, black-smiths, goldsmiths, weavers were the immigrant communities who settled in the town. The Boharas were the notable inhabitants of this group in Poona town and conducted the trade in iron, ironware and glassware.[35] Traders trading with grocery also belonged to the Maratha and Lingayat communities.[36] Members of Jain community were also busy in trading activity in capital town like Poona.[37] Even the

Brahmin community had its own leading merchants in the town.[38] Harikarna[39] was a famous merchant who dominated the trading activities in town of Poona in the 18th century. Some European merchants also lived in Poona and were engaged in commercial activities of the town.[40] Other members of this group were money lenders.[41] The bankers like Naik, Dixit-Patwardhan, Vaidyas, Tulshibagwale, Wakade, Wanwale, Biniwale,[42] etc. had settled in Poona town and by providing loans to different sections of urban society, they could exercise the influence over other groups in town. Dullabh Sheth was a famous banker in Poona who was popularly known as Nagar Sheth (leading merchant) of the town. His activities of money lending were extended to Lahore in the north and to Rameshwar in Southern India.[43] The close association of some of the bankers with ruling families of the Peshwas resulted in establishing matrimonial relations between them. Thus, for instance, a daughter of Dixit-Patwardhan, a leading banker in Poona town was married to Vishwasrao Peshwa.[44] The money lender derived much benefit from their association with the nobles or ruling families and got the right to collect the revenue or to collect other taxes from the people. The position of some of the bankers in Poona town rose to such an extent that they were employed as Pagedar i.e., the commander of troops by the Maratha rulers, while others became the saranjamdars and also the watandars (Patil) by purchasing the watan of Patil [45] Capital town as well as industrial places of Solapur,[46] Cheul, Jalnapur,[47] Chandwad were mostly populated, apart from the above groups, by a large number of weaving communities like Momin, Padamshalis, Khatris, Koshtis and Sakulsalis, etc. Other communities associating with the profession in Poona town which formed the larger section of urban population were the milkmen (Gawali), yer,[48] physicians,[49] gamblers,[50] masons, oilmen, shoemakers, saddlemakers,[51] blacksmiths,[52] goldsmiths, and potters etc.

Lastly, in towns, there was a group of labourers who belonged to different castes. Moreover, they were at the lowest level as far as their social and economic position is concerned,

A large number of them belonged to untouchable castes such as Mahars, Mangs, cobblers etc., and they were employed in houses by the Maratha feudatories and also by government officials in towns.[53] Some of them worked as marine labourers,[54] colies, watchmen, informers, etc. Slave labourers worked as servants in the houses of government officials,[55] in state factories,[56] and also in other departments of government.[57] The Hindu slaves belonged to the caste of goldsmith, carpenter, washerman, Kolis, gardener, blacksmith, shepherds etc., and Muslim slaves were the siddhis.

Harmony among Sub-groups

Unity of commercial groups can also be witnessed on the occasion when the government officers harassed them. Thus, for instance, the traders in Kasba Saswad such as leave vendors, oilmen, dyers, and others shut up their business against the oppressive measures of Deshmukh who collected illegal and excessive taxes from them.[58] So all the traders stood unitedly to fight against oppressiveness of government officers and defended their rights. The unity of inter-groups gave such a strength that it caused the government to order the concerned officer to stop the harassment of the traders.

It is obvious that all the social groups and sub-groups were based on rigidity of the caste system due to which they were prohibited from social intercourse, interdining and intermarriages etc. Besides other reasons, the main source of rivalries among inter-social groups in towns in Maharashtra was the attitude of imposing disabilities by one social group over the other.[59] Thus, a dispute between coppersmiths and Banias arose when the objection was raised by the former over their privilege of taking marriage procession through the market place by the latter.[60]

Similarly, other dispute arose between the coppersmiths, blacksmiths on the one hand and the potters on the other. In this case, the potters made the complaint of dispossessing their right of taking the bride and bridegroom riding on a horse in marriage procession to the government.[61] Such instances occurring in our records show how a sort of group tension was prevailed in urban society of those days. From the above analysis of urban social groups in Maratha country, it can be said that the people in towns seem to have divided into three categories such as rich, middle and poor. The members like bankers, rich traders, physicians and other professional men occupied middle position between the privileged group of Maratha Saranjamdars, or nobles and poor men of skilled workers, daily labourers in towns. They were the people who acquired the middle status in urban society in Maharashtra of pre-British period.

Urban Social Mobility

The urban society in Maratha country in the 18th century was marked with certain features like freedom to choose the place of domicile, freedom to gain a basic livelihood, freedom to have economic activities and also for mixing socially and lastly, the freedom to slaves in urban society etc. One of the important aspects of urban social mobility is the migration of the people from different places of the country to the urban localities. There is no doubt that the aspects such as urban migrations or freedom to choose the place of domicile or freedom to gain a basic livelihood etc., are inter-related aspects of urban social mobility. And in these respects, urban society in Maharashtra in the 18th century seems to be mobile. The people who had migrated from far off places in the country and settled at urban places in Maratha country, were the communities having skill of work. They were free to migrate from one place to another in order to get employment or to gain a basic livelihood. They had freedom to choose the place of domicile and there were no bindings at all about their settlements. We also find the instances wherein different groups of people in society like traders, skilled workers, bankers etc. shifted from different localities of India to urban centres in Maharashtra to find out the employment or to earn money. It is true that the people on large scale did not migrate from other places to the towns in Maharashtra, but the scale of migration from other localities into the cities like Bombay, Poona, Solapur, Yeola, Chandwad, Nagpur, Pen, Panvel, Cheul etc., was not at all negligible. Urban sources of income particularly trade, industry and banking played an important role in facilitating the mobility of urban classes of artisans, skilled workers, bankers, merchants in Maharashtra.[62] The trade of Bombay which increased enormously in the 18th century, provided an opportunity for social mobility to some traders, bankers and skilled workers to migrate from Surat and other parts of Gujrath to the city of Bombay.[63] It helped to encourage the ability of economic activities of several Bhandaries of Cheul, of the Banias, Parsis, Panchkalasis, Wadia families etc., who migrated from Gujrath and became immigrants in Bombay city[64] in the 18th century.

Likewise, trading activities in Poona, the capital city of the Maratha empire, also attracted numerous traders and skilled artisans to migrate to the city from northern and southern parts of India in the 18th century. The Boharas, who settled in Poona migrated from Ahmedabad, Aurangabad and Ahmadnagar. The Maheshwari Banias, Marwadi Banias, and Gujarathi Banias migrated from Rajasthan, Jodhpur, Sirohi and Gujrath respectively.[65] The weaving communities like Momin, Khetris, Salis, etc., who settled in city, came to Poona from Hyderabad, Nagpur and Paithan.[66]

Industrial activities of the urbanites, which resulted in rural-urban mobility were another means of urban mobility of our period. The activities of weaving industries, in Solapur and Yeola, attracted many trading and artisan families to migrate from other territories to the cities during the 18th century. Thus, the weaving communities like Khetri, Momin, Padamshalis, Niralis, Lingayat and non-Lingayat, Koshtis[67] etc., were the immigrants who migrated from Nizam's territory and Karnataka to Sholapur. The silk weaving industry at Yeola also attracted numerous silk weavers to migrate from Gujrat and Nizam's territory to the city.[68]

The money lending business also became a source of mobility for families of Vaidyas and Bhide who had migrated from neighbouring localities like Konkan[69] and Satara[70] to the capital city of Poona. The bankers also provided loan to the Peshwas who granted inam villages to them. Thus, the banking business contributed to the power and prestige of the Vaidya and Bhide families by getting the inam villages from the government.[71] It is interesting to note here that some part of profits earned by money lenders was utilised in constructing beautiful temples and also in extending patronage to learned scholars or mediciners[72] in urban centres.

Individual mobility in economic and political power dimensions was also not lacking in urban society of those days. Bugaji and Gangaji Naik who belonged to the immigrant community of Panchkalshi at Cheul received Anjur village in inam from the Maratha Government, with the title of Naik Sarpatel in consideration of their help given to the Marathas against the Portuguese in 1739 A.D. Others had occupied high position in society by acquiring the posts of Patels, Sarpatels and Desais for the services they rendered to the government.[73] We find another evidence showing interesting dimension and upward trend among the weavers, the immigrant community of Koshti in Poona city. Some weavers belonging to the group of Kadu Koshti had become well to do through the weaving craft. They had established matrimonial relations with their caste group at Karhkale in Sangamner pargana[74] who supposed themselves to be superior than the others. It is interesting to note that the group of Kadu Koshti in Poona who formerly did not have such matrimonial relations with the groups of their community in Karhale, could rise socially to their similar heights by attaining better economic position. Therefore, they could establish such social relations with them. These instances are enough to show a shift in upward direction of an individual in his social and political status which he acquired in urban society. At another level urban mobility can be inferred from the right of freedom, though in limited degree, enjoyed by the slaves in Maharashtra in the 18th century. The slaves could make themselves free on the request[75] or on the provision of substitute,[76] and thus enjoyed the right of freedom which is an important pre-requisite for mobility in any society. They could possess the property in form of land, houses,[77] and animals[78] etc. In some cases, some inam lands were also given to them by Maratha Government. Thus, for instance, Tapi and Jaini, the female slaves got the inam lands by the Peshwas when they had been set free.[79]

The freedom to individuals for mixing socially is another important aspect of urban mobility. Moreover, the rigidity of caste system did not allow the immigrant communities to mix socially with the native members of their castes. The immigrant communities who followed different customs were treated as outsiders in society by the native members of the same caste.

For instance, the immigrants like Parsis, Boharas, Banias etc., who had migrated to Poona settled in the cantonment and not in the city.[80] Similarly, native potters in Poona lived in Kasba peth whereas Pardeshi potters who had come from Rajasthan resided in Vetal and Ganj Ward.[81]

Moreover, there was also no interdining and no intermarriage between the native communities in Poona city and other corresponding immigrant communities. Likewise, the communities like Panchkalshis Prabhu in Bombay and their divisions of Sashtikar, Vasaikar at Pen, Panvel, Cheul, could neither eat together nor intermarry.[82] The lack of social contact among the immigrants and the natives could not bring any transfusion of skills and techniques between them. The social taboos also brought obstacles in the formation of one common guild of artisans of basket makers and of such other communities in the cities.[83] In this respect, the urban society in Maharashtra could not eliminate the social caste barriers and can be regarded as immobile. But we also come across examples of intercaste marriages though a few in number, which used to take place in urban society of those times. Thus, a weaver belonging to the group of Kadu

Koshti in Poona married to a female slave.[84]

A marriage between the slave-daughter and a dyer had taken place in 1776-77 in presence of a Kazi of Poona city.[85] Some lower groups of Maratha caste had established matrimonial relations with higher group of their caste.[86] In such circumstances, the lower caste groups by changing occupations or by associating with the members of higher castes,[87] attained social rank and consequently it led to the upward mobility of lower castes. Of course, the evidences of intercaste marriages are not given here to state that social mobility resulted in the elimination of caste system, but to understand the tendency of adjustment of urban society to the changing circumstances whereby different new sub-castes came into being.

Lastly, the rare cases of taking the children of the persons having intercaste marriages into their original caste or admitting them into the caste to which their fathers belonged, are also notable. For instance, the children who were born to a female slave from a Brahmin, after admitting them into their father's caste, were entrusted to the care of his wife.[88] And thus, the children after accepting as his legitimates got a place in the original community. Such instances certainly indicate the trends and process of urban social mobility better than tolerance of the period under review.

Professions and Occupations in Towns :
Physicians (Vaidyas)

Contemporary sources of our period relating to the taxes levied on different trading classes and others, show that a large number of people in 18th century Maharashtra were busy in earning their livelihood by following different professions. The persons expert in relieving the patients from their diseases were known as Physicians. They received the honour and high respect in the Maratha society. They were rewarded the grants of inam lands by Peshwa government when they cured the diseased men. Thus, for instance, a renowned physician like Sadashiv Bhat Nanal who cured the Chhatrapati was granted an inam of one Chavar of land at Nasarapur by the government.[89] Sometimes, the village was also granted in Inam to the physicians who possessed skill in the surgery or for their proficiency in the medicines.[90] It appears that physicians earned a lot on surgery. The prices of medicines were not fixed. It is interesting to note that the renowned physicians were patronised by the Peshwas and they were known as Rajvaidya. A medical practitioner was awarded a residential quarter by the Peshwa government and he was exempted from the tax to be levied on the fruit trees which grew in an area under his possession.[91] The physicians who opened a charitable dispensary for the poor, were granted a share of revenue by the government.[92] But if they failed in dispensing the medicines to the poor, the grant was discontinued.[93] Some of the physicians like Wasudev Bhat at Sangamner also received an allowance of rupees two hundred (hundred rupees for the cost of medicines and another hundred for his maintenance) by Peshwa government for dispensing medicines to the poorer. This profession was hereditary. So the allowance was continued to the son of physician even after the death of the father. In order to prepare the medicines, enough land with sufficient water for growing the medical herbs, was also provided by the government. The Peshwas and the Maratha nobles never appointed the physicians at villages or localities. But some of them were patronised at the court. They were also patronised by the Shinde, Holkar Sardars who granted them villages in inam.[94] There were some Gujarathi men who followed the proficiency of medicine at Poona.[95] We do not find a single evidence referring to private physicians of the Peshwas. But expert physicians from outside were invited for the need of the Peshwas and their family. Occasionally, the Portuguese renowned physician was invited for the military troops. He was honoured with by providing him palanquin.[96] Similarly, another renowned physician namely Bharmanna who lived at Hyderabad in the court of Nizam was brought to cure the diseased leg of Kashibai, the mother of the Peshwa.[97]

It appears that some of the physicians in Maharashtra

were expert and well trained in pharmacological knowledge. Usually, the medicines were very bitter. For instance, medicine administered to the patient, Govind Pant Patvardhan at Miraj, by Shivram Bhat, a physician who himself prepared it, could not be swallowed by the former, due to its bitterness,[98] We read in contemporary records that pearl, diamond, Suran,[99] gem and such other things were used as chemical materials for preparing the medicines.[100] Thus, the medicine called "Sannipat Bhairav Matra" was prepared by using pearls and jewels.[101] It appears that in the reign of Peshwa Madhavrao I, the medical department was established and different kinds of medicines were stored there. The raw materials required for preparing the medicines were brought from Surat[102] and Salesetle.[103]

In the early days of the 18th century, the Hindus accepted the teatment only from the Hindu physicians and they did not approach to Europeans. It is also evident that the European medicines were applied only when the Hindu medicines failed to cure the patients. A letter of Trimbakrao Pethe, addressed to Raghunathrao brings out the truth of this statement. It says that the Hindus were very much impressed by the Armenian doctors who used effective medicines for relieving the persons from their diseases.[104] The Peshwas also employed the British physician brought from Revdanda on monthly salary of rupees one hundred and fifty.[105] Portuguese physician like Don Antonio Jose Eirices, also stayed at the court of Shahu and acted as a spy. He sent the news to the Portuguese governor at Goa. Other Portuguese physician who provided medical aid to the Peshwa Madhavrao I, was Frei Liandro de Madre de Deos, the Catholic physician.[106] The physicians had to go to the places wherever they were called by the diseased persons.[107] They had to reach at the forts and provide medical treatment to prisoners kept in prisons.

Public Entertainers (Musicians, Singers and Dancers)

Dance, music, and drama were not only the means of

public entertainment of those times but also became a source of livelihood of a large number of people. It is a well-known thing that the King Shahu and some Maratha nobles were very much fond of music and also the fine arts. For his taste, the King Shahu gave an order to his nobles to send famous actresses from Delhi and other distant places in India to his royal palace.[108] The handsome female dancers were brought from Sironj, Karnataka and Konkan and earned a lot by following the profession of dancing at Poona, Satara and other places in Maratha country.[109] After the death of Shahu, a big number of dancers and musicians were regularly patronised by the Peshwas. Peshwa Nanasaheb was also fond of dance. So he sent his agent to Aurangabad to bring good dancers and singers at Poona.[110] Single group of dancing maidens was engaged for the entertainment of the nobles on twenty rupees as their monthly allowance.[111] The skilled and experienced artists were engaged in imparting lessons to other young girls in dance and music. The male and female singers and musicians received some amounts of rewards from the Peshwa government for the skill in their arts. The artists were also offered the clothes by the government.[112] On occasion of Hindu festivals the actors were honoured by giving them rewards.[113] It is to be noted that committing immoral conducts with dancing girls, was considered as crime. The Peshwas also patronised the male and female singers and actors at their court.[114]

A group of female dancers such as Chanda Vadankar, Panalekar, Asha Kolekar, Jaina, Maina Khedkar, Anandi Supekar, Mira Palkar, Ana Satarkar etc., was invited and their dancing was enjoyed by the Chhatrapati at Satara and also by the Peshwa on the occasion of offering a feast to the King by the latter.[115]

Sorcerers (Magician)

There were a few men in urban society who earned money by practising several magical tricks like causing evil spirit to be possessed by the women,[116] practising magic causing the human death,[117] or practising power to drive out evil spirits,[118] or harassing the persons by setting their houses on fire or destroying their property with the help of evil spirits[119] etc. It was believed by common people of those days that some women possessed by evil spirits due to the witchery practised by the men who could also possess the power to drive out evil spirit. In return they received some rewards also.[120] Another common feeling that prevailed in society of our period was the power of sorcery which caused to somebody's death.[121] Therefore, an inquiry was made by the Government officers regarding the persons who possessed the power over evil spirits. The offenders practising witchery making loss of human beings were arrested and sent into the prison.[122]

Writer

The profession of writing was followed by the learned men in Maratha society and also became the means of their livelihood. Gujrathi and Kanadi speaking men also engaged in this profession.[123] The writers who made the copies of different books also received the remuneration as prices of copies which were varied from two rupees to three rupees per thousand[124] pages. It appears that the rate of copying the valuable religious books was much higher than other ordinary books. Thus, for instance, the writer who made a copy of the Rigveda Samhita received an amount of twenty rupees as his remuneration.[125] But a copy writer of a Dnyaneshwari received only five rupees as its price.[126] Some book writers were also employed on annual salary of rupees one hundred.[127] A big volume running to thousands of pages was contributed by more than three writers and they received their remuneration by equally distributing the amount among themselves. The bankers like Tulshibagwale,[128] Chiplunkar etc.,[129] purchased a number of books which they kept in their private collection. They employed many men in writing or copying various books such as Sutsamhita, Brahma Gita, Dnyanyogkhand, Aprark, Madavi Parijat, Agnipuran, Adhyatma Ramayan and so on.[130]

The copies of other books like Gaya Mahatmya, Kedar Mahatmya, Shivpurana, Gadaparva, Sabhaparva, Madhya-sidhanta-Kaymudi, Geeta, Vedas, Ramayana, Bharat Champugrantha, Mudrarakashas, Prapanehsar, Kalidasa's Shakuntal, Prabodh Sudakar, Bhagwatpuran, Matsyapurana, Ratnavali, Manjari, Chhandogya Kirnavali, Panchop, etc. were made by the different writers of these days.[131] The writer, if he lost the original text, had to pay the price of manuscript to the owner. Thus, a writer when engaged writing a book for the banker like Chiplunkar, had to pay ten rupees as a compensation for the loss of the original text.[132]

Painter

The artists expert in paintings did not follow their profession just to make money, but also to show their special skills and talents. Painters engaged in drawing the pictures on walls, on the occasion of celebration of thread ceremony (Munj), were highly paid for their art.[133] Painters drawing pictures on paper were employed by the Peshwa Government on monthly salary of rupees thirty.[134] They were also provided with all material required for colouring.[135] The artists specialised in mural paintings were patronised by the Peshwa and some other Maratha nobles. A large number of experienced painters were engaged in Rajmala[136] paintings (Paintings illustrating ragas) which was very popular form of art of painting at Peshwa's court's of audience and in the residential mansions also.

Astrologers

Astrology was well flourished in Maharashtra of Peshwa period. Men and women in Maratha society believed in the fortunate or in unfortunate days. They had strong faith in omens and superstitions. So they always approached the astrologers before undertaking any project or new work. The Maratha rulers, their Peshwas and Maratha nobles also believed in augury and they consulted the astrologers to know auspicious time or unfortunate situation supposed to be created by individual's planets[137] for undertaking journey or for performing certain religious rites or for the entrance into newly constructed houses. An auspicious moment was sought to see any respected person. The Peshwas and Maratha nobles awaited and delayed their tasks whenever they did not find any auspicious time for starting new work.[138] The Peshwas always took the advice of the astrologers as to when the campaign was to be undertaken. Usually, the expeditions always commenced on an auspicious day. So many expert astrologers were patronised at the court of the Marathas. If the expedition could succeed on the same auspicious day, as was propitiated by an astrologer, the land in Inam was awarded to him by the Peshwas. For instance, we are told that when Sadashivrao Bhau defeated the Nizam, the enemy of the Marathas, at Udgir in 1769, the astrologer, Govind Dixit Patankar who sought the auspicious day for the same campaign, was granted a village Inam yielding five thousand rupees as annual income by the Peshwa.[139] Similarly, a astrologer namely Mahadev Narayan Pawaskar, at Poona was granted a piece of land for his foresighted information that Gangabai would give birth to a son on the day of the 7th Vaishaka Suddha.[140]

Betel-leaf Seller

A business in betel leaf was also in flourishing condition in Maharashtra, as a large number of Hindus and Muslims consumed betel-leaves in those days. Betel plants were grown in coastal land of Konkan territory. Especially, the land of Ratnagiri was useful and was brought under its cultivation.[141] Specialised community who followed the profession of selling betel leaves was known as Tamboli.[142] In every market town Tamboli had his own shop that was subjected to give five leaves to Shete on every day.[143] This profession was taxed by the government which collected twelve annas from hundred plants of the owner.

Gambler

Gambling which was subject to the government tax, was a favourite profession during the Peshwa period. Gambling played by men was not uncommon only in urban society but was also popular among rural people of our time. We have enough evidences to the fact that boys were also gambling in jungle.[144] The professional gamblers in town were not allowed to gamble without the permission of the Kotwal.[145] Other persons were not allowed to gamble by the Kotwal of the town.

Prostitute

The profession of prostitute was regarded as the meanest of occupations in Maratha society. The status of prostitute was considered as degraded in the society in the 18th century. Prostitute, as it was supposed impure, was not allowed to enter into the temple of Hindu god. For instance, two prostitutes in Poona town had to pay a fine of rupees two hundred as they went into the temple of Nageshwar Mahadev.[146] Prostitute had the liberty to take service where she liked.[147] A girl of four years old was purchased by the prostitute and she was brought up and then was trained for the profession. Usually, married women were not allowed by the government to become the prostitutes.[148]

Thief and Robber

The robbery, theft and dacoity, etc., followed by different communities in Maharashtra appear to be very common. The communal[149] tribes such as Bhils, Berads, Pendharis, Mang and Kolis, etc., were engaged in committing the plunders and theft. They were so expert in the profession that once they plundered the camp of Nawab very successfully.[150] On some occasions, the Berads performing the duty of guards also adopted the practice of dacoity.[151] The dacoity was not committed by a single person or a few men, but a band of forty or fifty persons were engaged in it and they altogether attacked the house of the wealthy person in town or village.[152] Besides the gangsters, there were also thieves who stole away the property of others. The robbers committing robbery also burnt the houses and extorted money from the people and harassed the traders who carried the merchandise. It is found that the villages were also infested with the robbers.[153] They were severally punished when they were arrested.[154] The persons who assisted the police officers in arresting the robbers were offered suitable rewards by the government.[155]

References and Footnotes

1. Parasnis, D.B., Poona in Bygone Days, p. 54.
2. Gadgil, D R., Poona, A Socio-economic Survey, Part II, p. 13.
3. Pune Nagar Sashodhan Vritta (PNSV) Part I, pp. 22-26.
4. Proceedings of the Indian History Congress Varanasi session (1969) "Aspects of the Zamindari System in the Deccan" by Nurul Hasan, p. 263.
5. Peshwa Diaries, IX, S. 204.
6. Ibid , IX, S. 207 and S. 209.
7. Richards, J. F., The Imperial Monetary System of Mughal India, p. 286.
8. Senapati Dabhade, Part I, BISM, quarterly Series, no. 81, p. 4.
9. Ibid., p. 5.
10. PNSV, Part I, pp. 59-60.
11. V K. Bhave, PKM, p. 32.
12. N.G. Chapekar, PS, Introduction, pp. 8-9.
13. Oturkar, R.V., PSAP, lekh no. 941.
14. Peshwa Diaries, VIII, Sanad 957.
15. Ibid., Sanads 1047, 1049.
16. Ibid., Sanad 955.
17. Ibid , Sanad 952.
18. PNSV, Bharat Itihas Sanshodhak Mandal (BISM) quarterly, Part I, p. 63.
19. Aitihasik Sankirna Sahitya, (ASS), Part VIII, p. 39.
20. Peshwa Diaries, VIII, Sanad 938.

21. PNSV, Part II, p. 161.
22. PSAP, Lekh no. 4.
23. V.T Gune, JSM, pp. 19-57.
24. ASS, I, p. 60.
25. S.V. Awalaskar, AP, pp. 8 & 6.
26 Gune, V.T., op. cit., p.57.
27. Ibid , p. 312. (Also see Pune Shaharatil Mahajan Va Nagaiseth, by D.R. Gadgil.)
28. G.S. Sardesai, PD, Part 31, Lekh no. 187.
29. Peshwa Diaries, VII, Sanad 712.
30. Ibid., III, S. 441.
31. Indian History Congress Proceedings, of the Seventh Session, Shetye-Mahajan by S.N. Joshi, pp. 287-88.
32. Ibid.
33. Ibid.
34. PNSV, Part IV, pp. 8-12.
35. ASS, VI, pp. 19-20.
36. AP, p. 8.
37. PNSV, II, p. 123.
38. Bhave, V.K., PKM, p. 32.
39. PNSV, Part III, BISM Quarterly no. 66, p. 218.
40 Parasnis, D.B., op. cit., p. 84.
41. PS, pp. 120-160.
42. Bhave, V.K., op. cit., pp. 32-33, and also see PNSV, Part I, BISM Quarterly, no. 54, p. 24.
43. Joshi, S.N , Para-Rashtranchya Darbaratil Marathyanchye Vakil, p. 27.
44. S.L. Vaidya, SVD, Part V, letter no. 10, dated 21st July, 1753.
45. PNSV, Part II, p. 93
46. Kakade, R.G., Socio-economic Survey of Weaving Communities in Solapur, p. 13.
47. Peshwa Diaries, VIII, S. 1076.
48. Ibid., VII, pp. 108-109.
49. Ibid., II, p. 129; also see Chapekar, N.G., op. cit., p. 221.
50. Ibid., VIII, p. 235.
51. Gadgil, D.R., op. cit., Part II, p. 32.
52. Peshwa Diaries, VI, S. 673.
53. Ibid., III, S. 130, S. 292 and VIII, S. 464.

54. Ibid., VI, S. 532.
55. Ibid., VIII, S. 958.
56. Ibid., VII, S. 747.
57. Ibid.. VII, S. 743, 747, and also Part VIII, S. 1045, S. 1096.
58. PSAP, Lekh no. 55, p. 40.
59. Sudha V. Desai, Social Life in Maharashtra Under the Peshwas, p. 40.
60. Ibid.
61. Peshwa Diaries, VIII, S. 1123.
62. Gazetteer of Bombay Presidency, Vol. IX and X, Part III, p. 33.
63. Ibid.
64. Gazetteer of Bombay City and Island, I, p. 154.
65. Grewal and Indu Banga, op. cit., pp. 99-101.
66. Ibid.
67. R.G. Kakade, op. cit., p. 13.
68. Gazetteer of Bombay Presidency, XVI, pp. 662-63.
69. SVD, V, letter no. 10.
70. PNSV, Part IV (BISM Quarterly series) 1952, p. 35.
71. SVD, V, letter no. 10.
72. PS, p. 10.
73. Gazetteer of Bombay City and Island, I, pp. 237-38.
74. Peshwa Diaries, VII, S. 763.
75. Ibid., S. 742.
76. Ibid., S. 748.
77. Ibid., VIII, S. 1108.
78. Ibid., VII, S, 746.
79. Ibid., VIII, S. 1108.
80. Gadgil, D.R., op. cit., II, p. 27.
81. Grewal and Indu Banga, op. cit., pp. 103-104.
82. Gazetteer of Bombay City and Island, I, p. 238.
83. Grewal and Indu Banga, op. cit., p. 104.
84. Peshwa Diaries, VII, S. 763.
85. Ibid., VIII, S. 1116.
86. PD, Part 43, p. 44.
87. Peshwa Diaries, VII, S. 763.
88. Ibid., VIII, S. 1118.
89. Sardesai, PD, Part 22, letter no. 225, p. 130.
90. Peshwa Diaries, II, pp 129-131; also see sanad nos. 208 and 211.

91. Ibid., II, p. 129.
92. Ibid., VII, S. 708.
93. Ibid., II, pp. 130-132.
94. Ibid., p. 129.
95. N.G. Chapekar, PS, p. 221.
96. PD, Part 22, letter no. 181.
97. PD, Part 40, p. 17.
98. PKM, by V.K. Bhave, p. 106.
99. Peshwa Diaries, II, p. 132.
100. PS, p. 221.
101. Peshwa Diaries, V, p. 245.
102. Ibid., II. p. 134.
103. Ibid., II, p. 132.
104. PKM, p 101.
105. PD, Part 22, letter no. 227.
106. P.S. Pissurlekar, PMR, p. 195 and p. 221.
107. Ibid., p. 224.
108. V.K. Bhave, PKM, p. 110.
109. Ibid., p. 110.
110. PD, Part 40.
111. PKM, p. 111.
112. Peshwa Diaries, VIII, S. 1151,
113. Ibid., VIII, S. 1149.
114. PKM, p. 14.
115. PD, Part 22, letter no. 226.
116. Peshwa Diaries, VIII, S. 924.
117. Ibid., VIII, S. 929; also see Vol. VII, S. 618.
118. Ibid., S. 926.
119. Ibid., S. 930.
120. Ibid., S. 924.
121. Ibid., VII, S. 929.
122. Ibid., VIII, S. 928.
123. N.G. Chapekar, PS, Introduction, p. 60.
124. Ibid., pp. 177-178.
125. Ibid., p. 177.
126. Ibid., p. 178.
127. Ibid.

128. Ibid., p. 179.
129. Ibid., p. 180.
130. PD, 22, letter no. 151, p. 94.
131. N.G. Chapekar, PS, pp. 177-180.
132. PD, Part, 22, letter no. 155.
133. PS, p. 300.
134. Peshwa Diaries, IX, S. 86.
135. Ibid., S. 85.
136. PD, Part 22, letter no. 179.
137. PKM, p. 116.
138. Ibid.
139. Ibid., p. 117.
140. Peshwa Diaries, IV Sanad 86, p. 89.
141. Ibid., VII. p. 1.
142. Ibid., VI, p. 329.
143. Ibid., II p. 212.
144. Ibid., VII, p. 199.
145. Ibid., VII, p. 247.
146. Ibid., VII, p. 326.
147. Ibid., VII, p. 244.
148. Ibid., VIII, p. 352.
149. Ibid., Vsss, pp. 89, 93 and 135.
150. Ibid., p. 89.
151. Ibid., p. 93.
152. Ibid., p. 92.
153. Ibid., p. 96.
154. Ibid., pp. 96, 97, and 99.
155. Ibid., p. 96.

Bibliography

Original and Secondary Sources

Original Sources

Marathyanchya Itihasachi Sadhane edited by V.K. Rajwade, Vols. I to 22, Poona, 1918.

Shiv Charitra Sahitya, Vols. 1 to 14.

Shiv Patrasar Sangraha, Vols. I to III.

Sambhajikalin Patrasar Sangrha.

Selections from the Peshwa Daftar, edited by G.S. Sardesai, 45 vols., Bombay Government.

Papers selected from the Vaidya Daftar, Vols. I to VI edited by S.L. Vaidya, Pune, 1944, 1945, 1949, 1951.

Selections from the Satara Raja's and Peshwa Diaries, Vols. 1 to 9 edited by Wad, G.C. and Parasnis, D.B., K.B. Marathe, and B.P. Joshi, Poona, 1905-1911.

Senapati Dabhade, Part I, BISM, Quarterly series no. 81.

Peshwaichya Sawalit—by Chapekar, N.G., Poona, 1937.

Peshwekalin Samajik Va Arthik Patra Vyavahara edited by R.V. Oturkar, Poona, 1950.

Tarabaikalin Kagad Patre, Part I, II, edited by Appasaheb Pawar, Kolhapur, 1969.

Shivshahi Portuguese Kagadpatre edited by S.S. Desai.

English Records on Shivaji, Poona, 1931.

Poona Nagar Sanshodhan Vritta, I to IV parts.

Public Original Consultation, Home Department Documents, 22 April 1789, (no. 25).

Selections from the Deccan Commissioner's Files (Peshwa Daftar) Period of Transition (1818-1826) by R.D. Choksey.

Report on the Territories conquered from the Peshwa by Mount Stuart Elphinstone Commissioner (1821).

Selections from the Records of Bombay Government.

Tours for Scientific and Economical Research Made in Gujrat, Kattiawar and the Conkuns in 1787-88.

Modern Works and Articles

Briggs, H.G., The Cities of Gujrashtra.

Bayly, C.A., Rulers, Townsmen and Bazars, North Indian Society in the Age of British Expansion 1770-1870.

Burton Stein, Peasant State and Society in Medieval South India, 1980.

Chithis, K.N., Glimpses of Medieval Indian Ideas and Institutions, Poona, 1974.

Fukuzawa, H., Land and Peasants in the Maratha Eighteenth century kingdom, Hitotsubashi Journal of Economics VI (i) June 1965.

Gadgil, D.R., Poona, A Socio-econmic Survey, 2 vols., Poona.

Gillion, K.L., Ahmedabad a study in Indian Urban History.

Grewal, J.S., Social change in Medieval India, General Presidential Address, Proceedings of Forty-fifth session of IHC, Annamalai. University, Annamalainagar, 1984.

Grewal, J.S., Urbanization in Medieval India, Urban History Association of India, Amritsar, 1982.

Grewal, J.S. and Indu Banga (ed.) Studies in Urban History, Amritsar, 1981.

Grover, B.R., Nature of Land Rights in Mughal India, IESHR, Vol. I, no.1.

Gokhale, B.G., Poona in the Eighteenth Century, Delhi, 1988.

Gupta, S.P., Agriculture and Agrarian Society Mid 17th century Information from Records of Pargana Manoadab iu Rajasthan, PIHC, Bodh Gaya, 1981.

Irfan Habib, The Agrarian System of Mughal India, Bombay, 1963.

Irfan Habib, The Technology and Economy of Mughal India, IESHR, Vol. XVII, no. 1.

Irfan Habib, The Peasant in Indian History, PIHC, Kurukshetra, 1982.

S. Kar, Agrarian System in Northern India, Bombay, 1990.

S. Nurul Hasan, Thougts on Agrarian in Mughal India, New Delhi, 1973.

S. Nurul Hasan, "Zamindars under the Mughals", Land Control and Social Structure in Indian History, London, 1969.

S. Nurul Hasan, Aspects of Zamindari System in the Deccan (1695-1707), PIHC, Varanasi, 1969.

Indu Banga, Agrarian Roots of Urbanization, The Case study of Medieval Batala, PIHC, Bodh Gaya, 1981.

Divekar, V.D., "Political Factor in the rise and decline of Cities in Pre-British India, Studies in Urban History.

Jain, K.C., Urbanization in Rajasthan (From 700 to 1200 A.D.) PIHC, Bodh Gaya, 1981.

Ghanshyam Lal and Devra (editors), Some Aspects of Socio-economic History of Rajasthan, Jodhpur, 1979.

Surendra Gopal, Commerce and Crafts in Gujrat 16th and 17th Centuries, New Delhi, 1975.

Narayani Gupta, Towers, Tanks and Temples : Some Aspects of Urbanisation in South India in the Eighteenth and Nineteenth Centuries, Urban History Association of India, Amritsar, 1983.

Kulkarni, A.R., "Social Mobility in 17th cetury Maharashtra," Maratha History, Seminar, 1974.

Kulkarni, A.R., Village Life in the Deccan in the 17th century, IESHR, Vol. IV, no. 1, Village Hakdars, PHC, Kurukshetra, 1982.

Kapur, Shiv Nath, Social Integration of Inter State Migrants in Kanpur, Agra, 1972.

Lallanji Gopal, Aspects of History of Agriculture in Ancient India, Varanasi, 1980.

Misra, S.C., Social Mobility in Pre-Mughal India, IHR, Vol. I.

Mahalingam, T.V., Readings in South Indian History, Delhi, 1977.

Moreland, W.H., The Agrarian System of Moslem India, Delhi, 1962.

Naqvi, H.A., Urban Centres and Industries in Upper India, 1556-1803, Bombay, 1968.

Ramendra Nath Nandi, Feudalization of State in Medieval South India, Social Science Probing Vol. I no. 1.

Hitesranjan Sanyal, "Social Mobility in Bengal; Its Sources and Constraints" : IHR Vol. II.

Sinha, P., Calcutta in Urban History, Calcutta, 1978.

Seminar on Urbanization, Surat, South Gujrath University, Surat, 1971.

Thakur Vijay Kumar, Social Mobility in Early Indian Urban Centres, A Theoretical Perspective, POHC, Forty First Session, Bombay, 1980.

Vatuk Sylvia, Kingship and Urbanization in North India,

Sharma, G.D., Land Revenue and Early Experiments in South Gujrat During the Second of the Eighteenth Century.

A case study of Pargana of Broach, PIHC, Bodh Gaya, 1981.

Gazetteers

Gazetteer of India, Maharashtra State History, Part II, Medieval Period, Bombay, 1972.

Gazetteer of India, Maharashtra State, Nasik District (Revised Edition), Bombay, 1975.

Maharashtra State Gazetteer, Jalgaon, District, Bombay, 1962.

Maharashtra State Gazetteer, Dhulia District.

Journals and Periodicals

Proceedings of Indian History Congress.

Indian Economic and Social History Review, Delhi.

Islamic Culture, Hyderabad.

Periodical of Maharashtra State Archives, ed. by V.G. Khobrekar, Bombay.

Rajwade Samshodhan Mandals' Quarterly (Dhule) Samshodhak.

Indian Historical Review, Delhi.

Bharat Itihas Somshodhak Mandal's Quarterly, Poona.

Bengal, Past and Present, Journal of Numismatic Society of India, Bombay.

Arthavijnana, Journal of Gokhale Institute of Politics and Economics, Poona.

Index